Eat and Stay Thin

Eat and Stay Thin

SIMPLE, SPIRITUAL, SATISFYING
WEIGHT CONTROL

by

Joyce Meyer

Harrison House
Tulsa, Oklahoma

EAT AND STAY THIN —
Simple, Spiritual, Satisfying Weight Control
ISBN 1-57794-144-6
Copyright © 1999 by Joyce Meyer
Life In The Word, Inc.
P. O. Box 655
Fenton, Missouri 63026

Published by Harrison House, Inc.
P. O. Box 35035
Tulsa, Oklahoma 74153

Contents

A Note to the Reader

Along with teaching from God's Word, this book contains practical suggestions for losing weight. Before making changes in your diet or exercise program it is very important to check first with your doctor.

Also, seek God to discover the particular course of action He wants *you* to take. The Lord may tell one person to fast, as He did with me at one point for a particular reason, but He may not want *you* to fast when you begin changing your eating habits. The Lord will guide you in the way most effective for you. Be open to His leading.

I have reviewed *Eat and Stay Thin* and find it to be excellent. It is my belief that if you follow the principles in the book and listen to what God says, you will be at your right weight.

Yvonne Goetsch, M.D.
Family Medical Care
Tulsa, Oklahoma

Introduction:

Freedom From Bondage!

Introduction:
Freedom From Bondage!

*I*n order for us to experience the fullness of the wonderful plan God has for us — the abundant life Jesus came to earth to give us (John 10:10) — it is important for us to be free from bondage, in whatever form, and the condemnation that often results. God does not want us to be in bondage to anything.

Whether the bondage takes the form of overeating, maintaining a certain weight or a pattern of reacting to circumstances with anger or fear, God has provided a way for us to become free through His Son Jesus. The Bible tells us, *If the Son therefore shall make you free, ye shall be free indeed* (John 8:36 KJV).

There is a great need for freedom in the area of bondage to food. Overweight people try to lose weight, then struggle to maintain a certain weight when (or if) they reach it. Underweight people work to gain weight. Many thin as well as overweight people live in bondage to being preoccupied with food — planning exactly what they will eat, how much and when — to maintain their size. Many people have struggled in this area for years, some people, for as long as they can remember.

One of the first areas in which God set me free was from the bondage of trying to control my weight. I am the right weight for my frame now, but through most of my childhood and early adult years, I was twenty to twenty-five pounds overweight and continued battling an extra ten to twenty-five pounds for years.

I spent my younger childhood disliking the way I looked, not feeling good about myself and dwelling on these types of thoughts. Being overweight became even more painful for me in my teenage years and early twenties. I felt as though I wasn't pretty and didn't look nice. I wasn't asked out on many dates because I was the girl who was asked out only if nobody else was left. That is a very hard thing to go through, so I understand how people who struggle in this area feel.

First I was in bondage to losing weight, then once I lost the weight, to keeping it off. I tried every imaginable diet and program until I finally found the one that works: God's program! The Lord led me to discover some truths that set me free from being controlled by food. I eat what I want, not what I think I ought to eat, without gaining weight or being deprived of certain foods.

People who constantly fight the battle with weight often feel bad about themselves. Whether it is an extra three, ten, twenty-five, fifty or 100 pounds they are trying to lose, or a certain number of pounds they are trying to gain, they usually have similar thoughts about their own appearance. They don't like the way they look. Even gaining three extra pounds for some people affects their confidence because their clothes don't fit right. People living in bondage to food, then to condemnation for failing to reach their weight goals, are not experiencing the peace and joy God wants for them on earth.

God's Kingdom *is righteousness, and peace, and joy in the Holy Ghost* (Romans 14:17 KJV). If you as a believer in Jesus Christ are experiencing condemnation, you are not experiencing the peace and joy God has made available to you through Jesus. Condemnation will stand between you and God like a giant wall to prevent you from receiving all that He wants to give you.

Romans 8:1 (KJV) tells us, *There is therefore now no condemnation to them which are in Christ Jesus....* John 3:17 (KJV) states, *...God sent not his Son into the world to condemn the world; but that the world through him might be saved.*

Hebrews 4:16 tells us how to approach God.

> Let us then fearlessly and confidently and boldly draw near to the throne of grace (the throne of God's unmerited favor to us sinners), that we may receive mercy [for our failures] and find grace to help in good time for every need [appropriate help and well-timed help, coming just when we need it].

Appropriate and well-timed help, coming exactly when we need it is the kind of help we want! The beginning of this Scripture tells us to fearlessly, confidently and boldly draw near to the throne of grace.

God doesn't want us to come before His throne in an attitude of fear, fearful to ask Him for the things we need without confidence that we are worthy to receive all that He has for us. He has made us worthy to receive

His help, and He wants to help us! He wants us to depend on Him. Second Corinthians 12:9 (KJV) speaking of the Lord says, *...my strength is made perfect in weakness....*

Jesus died on the cross to set us free from sin (1 Corinthians 15:3) and the condemnation that results. First John 1:9 (KJV) tells us, *If we confess our sins, he is faithful and just to forgive us our sins, and to cleanse us from all unrighteousness.* When we sin, we need to ask God for forgiveness then stop beating ourselves over the head with the sin. When we ask Him for forgiveness, He forgives us and we can forgive ourselves. By dwelling on how inadequate we thought we were, we are continuing to block what God has for us by not being open to receive from Him.

If you go before God's throne feeling bad about yourself, you will not be able to receive from Him in the great measure He wants to give to you. Condemnation will keep you from boldly going to God to obtain the very help you need to win over the bondage of struggling with your weight!

Freedom from condemnation is one of the major doorways to all the other blessings of God. It is important to have confidence in who we are in Christ to receive all the good things God has for us in order to be able to boldly obey and serve Him.

In struggling with their weight, people can fall into the deception of thinking their failures in meeting their weight goals make them unacceptable to God! Our weight has nothing to do with who we are in Christ. Our weaknesses have nothing to do with how acceptable we are to God. God has made us acceptable in spite of our weaknesses, no matter what they are, and wants us to let Him help us with them.

If we allow ourselves to slide into the pattern of thinking that our worth is based on how well we handle our weaknesses, we will reject and condemn ourselves. And, as we saw before, condemnation prevents us from boldly going to God to obtain the help we need!

In examining the subject of controlling your weight it is very important to continually remind yourself that God loves the person who is overweight just the same as He loves the person who is not overweight.

God accepts you and loves you unconditionally. He has put you in rightstanding with Him through what *He* has done by sending His Son, when you simply accept this salvation as the free gift it is. (See 1 Corinthians 1:30; Romans 5:17; Ephesians 2:8,9; Romans 10:9,10.)*

God loves you no matter what you weigh, but He wants you to be the right weight for you so that you can operate at your peak. He wants you to take care of your body to be in good health. If you wear out the body you have, you don't have another one stored in a drawer somewhere to pull out and use as a spare!

I had a desire on my heart for a long time to present a special message on why people are overweight or

---

* To receive Jesus as your Savior, see the prayer at the back of this book.

overeat. One day in a very short period of time, God gave me a list of reasons. I wrote them down on one of my bank deposit slips — all over the front and back. This book is based on them. You may recognize one or several of them as the reason, or reasons, food, or something else, is out of balance in your life. But it is important that you ask God to show you the specific reason or reasons (beyond the ones that seem obvious) why *you* are struggling in this area.

> Ask God to show you the real reason
> why you overeat or struggle
> with your weight.

John 8:31,32 (KJV) says:

Then said Jesus to those Jews which believed on him, If ye continue in my word, then are ye my disciples indeed; and ye shall know the truth, and the truth shall make you free.

When Jesus reveals a truth to you, that truth will make you free. My general manager, Roxane, weighs only about 93 pounds, but she discovered a truth about her eating habits that set her free from a form of bondage.

Roxane and her husband, Paul, live with us. My husband, Dave, and I travel quite a bit, and when we are out of town, Roxane and Paul take care of our house and office. Roxane has good eating habits now, but when she and Paul first moved in with us, she didn't eat at the same time as everyone else or ate junk food later instead of a meal.

Sometimes she didn't eat all day. Then during dinner, saying she wasn't hungry, she picked at her food and pushed it around on her plate. But as soon as everyone else finished eating, she started in and ate her whole meal. Sometimes instead of eating dinner, she ate an entire regular-sized bag of potato chips or a half bag of pretzels.

Roxane told me after she and Paul were first married, she cooked a good meal for him and basically did the same thing. She ate a little bit during dinner, but after he was done, then she really started eating. I didn't understand why she ate like this and neither did she. To find out the reason, Roxane went before God and asked Him.

God showed her that when she was growing up there was often strife at mealtimes. Because of that, she associated eating with disturbance and had no desire to eat in a family setting.

On another occasion when she and one of her sisters were talking about Roxane's habit of eating almost nothing but candy bars and other junk food in high school and college, they learned another reason for Roxane's eating habits. They recalled that most of the pleasant family times were on the weekends. The whole family, with sixteen children, sat in the family room, watched TV and ate popcorn on Saturday night, and on

Sunday, ate candy their dad went out to buy for them that day. God showed them the main times they connected pleasure with food were on the weekends when they ate junk food in that fun setting.

Once Roxane understood the reason for her eating habits, she said, "Well, I don't have to eat that way anymore!" She immediately began eating her meals with everyone else and selecting more nutritious foods.

Many times when we see the truth, we also see a simple change we can make to correct a problem, or we discover the situation and the solution are much less complicated than we imagined. As we see in 2 Corinthians 11:3 (KJV), the devil likes to complicate our lives to keep us distracted from seeing the simplicity that is in Christ: *But I fear, lest by any means, as the serpent beguiled Eve through his subtilty, so your minds should be corrupted from the simplicity that is in Christ.*

People who study the principles of sound nutrition sometimes find themselves powerless to put those principles to work effectively in their lives. Many people who try to follow different diets find they are powerless to keep all the rules and regulations, or do follow the diet strictly, but without seeing the long-range results they desire.

Rather than trying in our own strength to follow a list of rules and regulations to control our weight, we can control the eating problem in the same way we solve all our other problems: by drawing on the power of the Holy Spirit and walking in faith!

The Holy Spirit leads us into nothing but victory and freedom. And when God gives us a plan, that plan will work!

I believe the twelve reasons people overeat or are overweight given in this book will open doors of understanding to you. Whether God shows you one or several reasons why you struggle in this area, rejoice in the truth! Then determine to let Him use the scriptural teaching in this book to give you the strength, wisdom and power you need to apply the practical teachings in it about nutrition and food.

I believe and have thanked God in advance that as you read this book, He will do a mighty work in your life to set you free from bondage.

Let Jesus set you free! And John 8:36 (KJV) tells us, *If the Son therefore shall make you free, ye shall be free indeed.*

Part 1

Freely Eat

1

The Flesh Wants To Do Crazy Things!

1

The Flesh Wants To Do Crazy Things!

*And the Lord God commanded the man,
saying, You may freely eat of
every tree of the garden.*

GENESIS 2:16

*G*enesis 2:16 was one of the first Scriptures God used to bring about a major change in my life when I first began to read and study His Word. Applying that Scripture brought victory in an area I had struggled with since childhood — controlling my weight.

When the Lord told the man, ...*You may freely eat of every tree of the garden,* He was saying, "You may freely eat of everything I have put here for you to eat." In other words, we are free to eat!

Once when I was teaching this subject, I asked the congregation to repeat after me, "I am free to eat!" It was amazing but not surprising to see the fear that crossed many of their faces. So many people who struggle with their weight have a fear of food because in the past it has mastered them instead of them mastering it.

They think, "Free to eat? *What if I get fat?*"

One thing that keeps people from reaching or maintaining a weight that is right for them is fear. They are in bondage to fear without realizing it — fear of "being fat" and fear of food! When they are afraid that anything they put in their mouths carries the potential for "making them fat," they would much rather follow the list of rules and regulations in a diet than have liberty. In following the strict rules of a diet, they feel secure they will be able to control their weight. But usually the opposite happens. Their diet plans often end in disappointment, failure and another weight gain because they are trying to be their own "keeper." They are trying to take care of themselves in their own strength rather than drawing on the Lord's strength.

Psalm 121:5 says, *The Lord is your keeper....* His plans for us work! The way to become free from living in bondage to food and being enslaved to diets is to start learning how to genuinely follow the leading of the Holy Spirit. He will always lead you into victory and freedom, not into gaining weight. On God's "Diet Plan" you eat what you want without gaining weight!

One of Satan's main tools is deceit. People who clearly hear and follow the leading of the Holy Spirit in other areas don't realize they are in bondage to fear in the area of controlling their weight. Fear keeps them from stepping out in faith in the power of the Holy Spirit to experience victory in this area. Without realizing it, they actually believe that controlling their weight is one area in which following the leading of the Holy Spirit and drawing on His power don't work!

GODLY RESTRAINTS

When you are overweight, you almost constantly think about your weight. Little thoughts about it almost seem to hang onto your head, following you around everywhere you go, constantly on your mind. Hearing what God is trying to guide you to do when you are constantly thinking about your weight is very difficult!

Being overweight, depending on the severity of it, dictates to you in many instances what you can wear, where you can go, what kind of chair you can sit in, car you can drive, sports you can play or other activities in which you can participate. When your activities are restricted because of your weight, you can develop all kinds of problems in your personality. You can miss developing deep relationships with people, and you can block what God is trying to communicate with you by putting up all kinds of defense mechanisms. God does not want His children to live below the level He has planned. He wants to lift you to heights you never thought possible!

As we have seen, Genesis 2:16 tells us, ...*You may freely eat of every tree of the garden.* Genesis 2:17 reveals what *freely eat* means.

> But of the tree of the knowledge of good and evil and blessing and calamity you shall not eat, for in the day that you eat of it you shall surely die.

To be free does not mean to live without restraint or in excess.

In God's terms, freedom does not mean the liberty to give in to the desires of the flesh. It means the liberty to be led by the Holy Spirit. (Romans 8:12-14.)

From what we are told in the Bible, the Garden of Eden was a very beautiful, bountiful place. It was filled with trees that produced all kinds of fruits. I am quite sure that since they were natural, they were much more tasty than anything we have today. Because there was no corruption in the earth, everything that came from it was full of wonderful vitamins and nutrients. So everything was much more satisfying than it is now.

Genesis 1:31 tells us, *And God saw everything that He had made, and behold, it was very good (suitable, pleasant) and He approved it completely....* I believe the fruits from the trees in the garden were extremely good-looking. Their very appearance made them appealing to the eye.

Into this garden, God placed the man and woman He had created, telling them, "You may freely eat of the fruit of any of these trees." So when Adam and Eve got hungry, they just reached up and picked something and ate it. But I don't believe for a moment that they ever overate, because they were led by the Spirit of God.

They ate when they got hungry. They quit eating when they were comfortable. Between times they probably never thought of food; it was never on their minds.

That is the way God has always intended. Food was there for the taking when it was needed, but it was not the constant focus or ultimate goal of life as it so often is today.

EAT RIGHT, FEEL RIGHT

God told Adam and Eve, "You can eat all the other fruits you want, but leave this one alone." That is the same message He is giving us today: "You can eat all of the good things I have provided for you, but it is going to be better for you if you leave certain things alone."

All of us know the things in our life God has told us to leave alone because they are not good for us or don't agree with us. For me, caffeine is one of those things.

For years I drank regular coffee with no problem. There was probably nothing I enjoyed more, especially in the morning. I looked forward to getting up early and spending time with the Lord over a cup of fresh, hot coffee. I loved my coffee.

Then all of a sudden some time ago I noticed that the caffeine was not agreeing with my system anymore. So I tried drinking half regular coffee and half decaffeinated. When that didn't ease the problem, I tried decreasing the regular coffee and increasing the decaf. I did everything I could think of to hold onto just a little bit of caffeine. I finally had to give it up altogether. Coffee has never tasted the same to me since.

I am always trying out different brands and types of coffee without caffeine, but most of them never taste good to me. So God has shown me that while I am free to consume many things, coffee with caffeine is not one of them.

I have learned that good health is more important to me than good coffee. I would rather feel great than feel miserable.

There is nothing worse than going through life feeling bad all the time. If we are honest, we know whether we are eating the right things or not. We also know whether we are carrying too much weight or not. We know because when we eat the wrong things or put on extra pounds we just don't feel right.

God has placed an anointing upon each of us, and He wants us to operate in that anointing. There is something He wants us to do. To do it, we must take care of our bodies, the house we live in. We have to eat and drink properly, get enough rest and exercise, and keep our weight down to what is right for our frame.

To be all that God intends for us, we must be delivered and set free from our preoccupation with food.

FOOD IS NOT THE PROBLEM

I know that there is nothing better for them than to be glad and to get and do good as long as they live;

And also that every man should eat and drink and enjoy the good of all his labor — it is the gift of God.

ECCLESIASTES 3:12,13

I am not saying that we should not enjoy food. God wants us to enjoy what we eat. Food prepared properly and eaten in the right amounts can be one of the most enjoyable things God has given us.

I love to eat out frequently. After I have finished working hard in a conference, one of the things I look forward to is going out to dinner. I love to just sit in a nice restaurant and relax and have a good time with other people. But I cannot stand to leave that restaurant so full I can hardly move or even breathe.

There are many things that are a blessing if done in moderation, but if done in excess they can become a curse. Eating is one of those things.

Food is not the problem. It's what we do with food that becomes the problem. That's why we need to learn to keep everything in our lives — especially our eating — in proper balance.

DEAL SERIOUSLY WITH A SERIOUS PROBLEM

When you sit down to eat with a ruler, consider who and what are before you;

For you will put a knife to your throat if you are a man given to desire.

PROVERBS 23:1,2

In this passage the Holy Spirit is obviously not saying that if we overeat we are to cut our throat! What He is saying is that if eating is a problem in our lives, we are to take that problem seriously and deal with it wisely.

I believe that food is more of a problem than many of us want to admit. This Scripture on the seriousness of eating is like the passage in Matthew 18:8,9 where Jesus said, *And if your hand or your foot causes you to stumble and sin, cut it off and throw it away from you.... And if your eye causes you to stumble and sin, pluck it out and throw it away from you....*

Recently someone told me about a woman in a church who felt that she had lusted with her eye, so she actually plucked it out of the socket. That kind of thing aggravates me. It is just the kind of deception that Satan leads people into.

Please do not misunderstand this Scripture. In it Jesus was not saying that we are to literally cut off our hand or pluck out our eyes. He was using a figure of speech to say that we are to take sin seriously and deal with it seriously. If we don't, we will never be truly free.

RESTRAIN YOURSELF

When you go out to dinner with an influential person, mind your manners; don't gobble your food, don't talk with your mouth full.

And don't stuff yourself; bridle your appetite.

PROVERBS 23:1,2 MESSAGE

In this version of Proverbs 23:1,2 there is a heading which reads, "RESTRAIN YOURSELF."

According to verse 2, we are to bridle our appetite. A bridle is a restraint. We are to bridle or restrain ourselves, not wait for somebody else to do it for us. We can do it with the help of the Holy Spirit.

DON'T DIE — LIVE!

For if you live according to [the dictates of] the flesh, you will surely die. But if through the power of the [Holy] Spirit you are [habitually] putting to death (making extinct, deadening) the [evil] deeds prompted by the body, you shall [really and genuinely] live forever.

For all who are led by the Spirit of God are sons of God.

ROMANS 8:13,14

I am so glad we don't have to do all the things the Bible tells us to do all by ourselves. There is such a wonderful life available to us if we will learn to live in the Spirit and not in the flesh.

The Bible tells us plainly that if we walk in the flesh we are going to experience all kinds of death. But if we walk in the Spirit, we are going to experience joy, peace, victory, and life in all its abundance as we see God's plan for us develop and unfold in our daily lives. It is well worth it to walk in the Spirit and not in the flesh.

The Bible tells us if we habitually say, "No," to the demands that our bodies make upon us and, "Yes," to the Spirit of God, we will be truly and genuinely alive.

Did you know there is a voice of the flesh and a voice of the Spirit? Many of the things the voice of the flesh tells us to do are just crazy. It tells us to eat when we are not hungry, to keep eating when we are full, to eat things we know are going to make us sick.

Have you ever eaten something you knew you were allergic to, something you knew was going to make you break out in a rash or have stomach problems or a headache? Why did you go ahead and eat it anyway? Why did you listen to your body rather than to the Spirit?

"...The spirit indeed is willing,
but the flesh..."[1] *wants to do crazy things!*

Many of the things our carnal flesh wants us to do are just crazy! When we obey the dictates of the flesh, we eat when we aren't hungry, eat more when we are already full and eat certain foods that could make us sick. Some people even eat some foods while fully expecting to have an allergic reaction!

We can live according to what our carnal flesh tells us to do, or we can live through the power of the Holy Spirit to put to death the dictates of the flesh. (See Romans 8:13,14.)

It's like having a crazy man living inside of us!

We know that is true. We know our body talks to us and tells us to do all kinds of stupid, idiotic things:

"Please don't make me get out of bed." "Please don't make me clean the house." "Please don't make me exercise." "Please stop at that donut shop and get me some jelly donuts." "Please give me coffee with caffeine in it, even though it's going to make me a nervous wreck."

We must not listen to our natural mind. We must listen to what the Spirit of God says. Through the power of the Holy Spirit within us, we must learn to say no to ourselves and yes to God so the fullness of God's plan for us can be manifested in our lives.

2

Birthright Sold for a Bowl of Stew

2

Birthright Sold
for a Bowl of Stew

*And Esau said to Jacob, I beg of you, let
me have some of that red lentil stew to
eat, for I am faint and famished! That is
why his name was called Edom [red].*

*Jacob answered, Then sell me today your
birthright (the rights of a firstborn).*

*Esau said, See here, I am at the point of
death; what good can this birthright do me?*

*Jacob said, Swear to me today [that you
are selling it to me]; and he swore to
Jacob and sold him his birthright.*

*Then Jacob gave Esau bread and stew of
lentils, and he ate and drank and rose up
and went his way. Thus Esau scorned his
birthright as beneath his notice.*

GENESIS 25:30-34

What was Esau really saying? "I'm so hungry I feel like I'm going to fall down and die. Please give me some of that stew because I need it to live."

Jacob answered, "I'll give you the stew if you'll give me your birthright in return."

Today the rights of the firstborn are not understood as they were in biblical times. In those days the firstborn son received a double portion of the inheritance and became head of the family. The rights of the firstborn were not something anyone wanted to let go of easily. Yet Esau was willing to sell his firstborn right for a bowl of stew — just because his body was screaming at him, "I want something to eat! I'm going to die if you don't feed me!"

Do you realize how foolish Esau was? He could not possibly have died of hunger in one day. He allowed his body to dictate to him, and the result was the loss of his greatest gift.

GOD'S KINGDOM IS NOT FOOD

[After all] the kingdom of God is not a matter of [getting the] food and drink [one likes], but instead it is righteousness (that state which makes a person acceptable to God) and [heart] peace and joy in the Holy Spirit.

ROMANS 14:17

I think many of us today sell our birthright for a bowl of stew or a box of donuts or a pizza.

What do I mean?

As the children of God we are entitled to certain rights. For example, as we see in this verse, we have a right to righteousness, peace, and joy in the Holy Spirit. Yet many of us who fight the weight battle all the time experience, not a sense of righteousness, peace and joy, but a sense of condemnation.

I can gain three pounds and feel condemned by it, which also affects my sense of confidence. My weight gain causes me to constantly think about how much I need to lose and how I am going to do it. Before I realize it, food is on my mind all the time.

It's not necessary to be a hundred pounds overweight for food to become a problem. There are many thin people who have to deal with this issue all the time. The reason is that we live in a food-oriented society today — and Christians are some of the worst "food addicts" in the world! We can hardly get together without eating.

A friend of mine tries to watch her weight but has a hard time of it because of her ministry. When you are a preacher, after services everybody wants to invite you out to eat in a restaurant or over to their house for a home-cooked meal. You have to be fighting off some kind of food offer all the time.

This lady made a good point. She said, "Everywhere I go to minister, to those in the meeting it's a special occasion. Afterwards, they want to celebrate with some kind of fancy meal or rich treat like pie. But to me, it's just another meeting, like those I go to every night. I know that if I have a big meal or a fattening dessert every time I preach or minister, I'll end up wearing it!"

Years ago my husband and I made the decision that when we go somewhere to minister, we won't go out and eat after the service. We have to tell people, "We don't mean to be rude or hurt your feelings, but we just can't accept your kind invitation." There are several reasons.

For one thing, Dave and I are now at the age where we need to get a full night's sleep. I have learned that I just don't function well on three or four hours of sleep. To be honest, if I go without enough sleep a few nights in a row, it makes me sick.

Another reason is that I don't sleep well after a big meal. I toss and turn and have nightmares. The next morning when I wake up, I don't feel well. My clothes don't fit me right, and I just don't feel good about myself.

I want to feel right. I want to feel good about myself. I want to be free. So I have decided that I am not going to sell my birthright for a bowl of stew or a piece of pie or anything else — even when it is offered by the best of people in the most loving manner for the most wonderful reasons. Although it's hard sometimes, I have learned to "just say no."

On rare occasions we do accept an invitation to go out after a service, but we go because we want to, not because our flesh, or someone else, is demanding it. It is not the "occasional liberties" that get us into trouble; it is allowing the flesh to rule that brings bondage and loss of victory.

Dave and I usually eat something after a service. We keep fruit, plain yogurt, vegetables and dip and other nutritious, yet nonfattening, foods in our hotel room. We normally eat in the early afternoon before our conference sessions, and by the late evening we need to eat something. It is not eating that is the problem, it is the choice of food and the amount of it selected that can become a problem.

If You Know What's Good For You...

Everything is permissible (allowable and lawful) for me; but not all things are helpful (good for me to do, expedient and profitable when considered with other things)....

1 Corinthians 6:12

As Christians, we have a right to peace and joy, not guilt and condemnation. That doesn't mean that we are not to enjoy food or any of the other good things that God has wonderfully created and provided for us. It just means that we are not to overindulge.

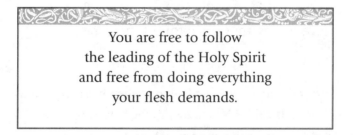

You are free to follow
the leading of the Holy Spirit
and free from doing everything
your flesh demands.

For example, it is not against the law for me to drink coffee. I am not going to hell just because I drink a cup of coffee with caffeine in it. I won't lose my salvation just because I eat a piece of pie every night at bedtime. But I know that although those things are lawful to me, they are not good for me.

Somewhere along the line we have got to get smart enough to know what's good for us. There are some things that we can get by with when we are young that we can't get by with later on in life.

Dave and I have a son who used to eat a lot of junk food when he was young. We tried to tell him numerous times, "David, please don't eat that stuff, it's not good for you."

"Oh, it's all right," he would say. "I feel fine."

"Yes, son," we would answer, "but you're young. One of these days when you get older your bad eating habits will start to cause you problems."

That is a lesson we all have to learn in life. If we mistreat our bodies, sooner or later there will be a price to pay. The sad part is that often by the time we realize what is happening, we have done so much damage we may have to pay that price for a long time.

Before It's Too Late

For you understand that later on, when he *[Esau]* wanted [to regain title to] his inheritance of the blessing, he was rejected (disqualified and set aside), for he could find no opportunity to repair by repentance [what he had done, no chance to recall the choice he had made], although he sought for it carefully with [bitter] tears.

Hebrews 12:17

Like Esau, sometimes we are so foolish, we get ourselves into all kinds of trouble. We mistreat our bodies until we realize what we have done to ourselves, and then we expect God to work a miracle to get us out of the mess we have made.

I see it all the time in my ministry. People abuse their bodies until they are a wreck, and then come to a meeting like ours looking for a miracle.

God does have mercy on His children, and I am sure that many people do get miraculous healings. But it is also true that many of those people suffer for a long time before finally receiving that miracle cure.

Miracle healing is wonderful, but it is not God's best. God wants His people to walk in wisdom so they don't have to fall into misery and pain before they come to their senses, which may sometimes come too late. It is better to live wisely and not need continuous miracles, than to live foolishly and always need a miracle to get out of trouble.

I am sharing these things with you because I know what I am talking about. I am not just theorizing. I have had experience in this area. God has been healing and restoring me over a period of time, and I am grateful for that healing and restoration. But that was not God's best for me. His best for me was to have avoided all that misery in the first place. That's what I am trying to help you do.

Not long ago my son David said to me, "You know, Mom, I'm going to have to stop eating some of this junk food. I'm not feeling as good as I used to."

Since he is still young, he is learning soon enough so that he will be okay. It's not too late to undo the damage he was causing by his bad eating habits.

When people are young, they think they can get by with anything, that nothing they do will cause them any problem. They think they can eat anything they want and never have to pay a price for it. At that age, their metabolism may be so active they can eat junk food and still feel good and function well. But sooner or later that situation changes. The sad part is that sometimes they learn too late.

Not long ago my daughter put on an outfit that someone had given her. It used to fit her well, but this time it was too tight across the hips. She got mad and threw it on the floor.

"I will not be overweight!" she yelled. Then she asked, "What's going on with my body?"

All her life she was the type who could eat anything she wanted and still stay slim and trim. Now she was getting closer to thirty and things had begun to change.

Obviously, thirty is not some magical number at which point everybody starts to become overweight. But usually about that time there is a difference in lifestyle which brings about changes in the body.

My daughter is not running around doing all the things she used to do. Her lifestyle is more sedentary now. She sits a lot, and when we start sitting we can't afford to eat as much as we did when we were more active. Also our metabolism tends to slow down, causing our bodies to put on excess pounds — usually in all the wrong places.

I personally noticed a real change in my body around the age of forty and again at fifty. At both of those plateaus in my life I gained two pounds. They suddenly seemed to come from nowhere. My eating had not changed, but my weight did. It really frustrated me for a long time until I finally faced facts that my body was changing. My metabolism was probably changing, and if I wanted to maintain my weight I would need to change something in my eating.

We can make minor changes that will help us maintain our weight as we reach the forties and fifties. I did things such as use less butter, or in many instances, skip it altogether. I also eliminated fried food at least ninety-five percent of the time, chose sugar-free drinks and avoided eating late at night.

As we get older, we have to expect changes in our bodies. That's why we have to start making changes in our lifestyle, especially in our eating and exercise habits. We have to start taking authority over our bodies rather than allowing our bodies to dictate to us.

3

Free To Serve

3

Free To Serve

*...Everything is lawful for me, but
I will not become the slave of anything
or be brought under its power.*

1 CORINTHIANS 6:12

The power of God is available for so many practical areas of our lives.

If we are not to become the slaves of anything or be brought under its power, we must set our faces like flint and dig in both heels. We have to be determined and say, "I will not be a slave to food or drink — to donuts, to pie, to potato chips, to fast-food hamburgers, to coffee, to soda pop, or to anything else. I am going to be free to be led by the Holy Spirit in every area of my life."

I want you to know that God cares about you and your body. He cares about your appetite and the struggles you have with it. He wants you to know what to do to bring your body and its appetite into submission.

EVERY GOOD ATHLETE EXERCISES RESTRAINT

Now every athlete who goes into training conducts himself temperately and restricts himself in all things....

1 CORINTHIANS 9:25

When the Bible says that an athlete restricts himself in all things, it means that he exercises self-control. He pays attention to everything in his life that might affect his performance on the court, course, or field. When he is in training, he watches what and how much he eats and drinks, how much rest and recreation he gets and how his body responds in practice.

The *King James Version* says that he is temperate in all things. To be temperate is to be moderate.

If we are going to get into condition to serve the Lord, we need to learn to practice moderation in all things. We need to exercise self-restraint in our conversation, in our diet, in our spending, in our time, in every area of our lives.

Why?

So we will not be disqualified in the race of life as unfit for service.

FIT FOR SERVICE

...They do it to win a wreath that will soon wither, but we [do it to receive a crown of eternal blessedness] that cannot wither.

Therefore I do not run uncertainly (without definite aim). I do not box like one beating the air and striking without an adversary.

But [like a boxer] I *buffet* my body [handle it roughly, discipline it by hardships] and subdue it, for fear that after proclaiming to others the Gospel and things pertaining to it, I myself should become unfit [not stand the test, be unapproved and rejected as a counterfeit].

1 CORINTHIANS 9:25-27

Sometimes Christians read this passage and think Paul was saying, "I *buffet* [buf-FAY] my body!" It's the same spelling but a different pronunciation.

Although the Christian buffet is often the biggest thing in the church, Paul did not "buf-FAY" his body. What he did was buffet [BUF-fit] it — handle it roughly, discipline it with hardships, and subdue it.

Why?

To assure that after preaching the gospel to others, he himself would not be found unfit, unable to stand the test, unapproved and rejected.

If we are to be fit for service to the Lord and His Kingdom, we must do what Paul did. We must exercise restraint and self-control. We must discipline our bodies, keeping them under our command and authority. To do that, we must be aware of the twelve reasons people overeat or become overweight. That's why the rest of this message is not going to be spiritual, but practical. I am going to try to give you some information that will save your life.

Part 2

The Truth Will Make You Free!

Twelve Reasons Why People Overeat

Reason 1:

Lack of Knowledge

Reason 1:
Lack of Knowledge

*My people are destroyed
for lack of knowledge....*

HOSEA 4:6

WHAT YOU DON'T KNOW
WILL MAKE YOU OVERWEIGHT!

The number one reason for destruction in the lives of God's people is a lack of knowledge. They just don't know — and despite the popular saying, what they don't know *does* hurt them. This rule applies in natural areas as well as in spiritual areas.

In regard to eating, lack of knowledge leads to poor food choices. Food with high fat, salt, calorie, and cholesterol content is the culprit behind many an overweight body.

Stated another way, many people overeat or become overweight simply because they don't have proper understanding of what they are putting in their bodies. They fill themselves with foods that have no nutritional value so they do not satisfy their real hunger. As a result, they go around constantly looking for something to eat because they don't feel satisfied.

GET EDUCATED

For I do not want you to be ignorant....

1 CORINTHIANS 10:1

If you are going to avoid this problem, get educated. Know what you are putting in your body. Read books on nutrition. Study the information on the back of the boxes, cartons, and bags in which your food is packaged. Almost all foods have to display this information for the consumer. Learn to read what it says and interpret what it means.

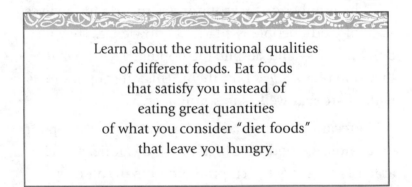

Learn about the nutritional qualities
of different foods. Eat foods
that satisfy you instead of
eating great quantities
of what you consider "diet foods"
that leave you hungry.

In our ministry, we receive a lot of complimentary fruit baskets. Often those baskets have more than fruit in them. Many times there are candies and nuts and other kinds of treats mixed in with the fruit. We once received a fruit basket that had in it a huge chocolate bar with a cherry-flavored liquid center. Another had a tiny box of chocolate truffles with cream centers.

I told my daughter, "I'll keep the fruit, but get the other stuff out of here. Give it to someone else."

She began to read to me the back of the packages describing how much fat and how many calories were in the chocolate bar. It was bad, but it wasn't terrible. Then she started reading what was in the truffles, and it was shocking. Four tiny little pieces of candy had twenty-five grams of fat!

"Wait!" I said to her. "Just throw it away! It would be a sin to give that to anybody."

I wouldn't have known what was in that candy if she hadn't read me the nutrition label.

It is amazing what you will turn down if you will just start reading the back of the package to see what you are about to put in your body. Yet many people eat all kinds of things like that and never even bother to read the label. That is part of what God means when He says that His people are destroyed because of a lack of knowledge.

When you go to eat in a fast-food restaurant, ask for a nutrition statement of the foods on the menu. If you are health conscious or trying to lose weight, you will think twice before you order that double cheeseburger with special sauce and the works on it, plus an order of French fries to go with it. When you discover you are about to swallow seven to eight hundred calories and sixty-five grams of fat, you might just change your mind!

GET OFF
THE DIET-GO-ROUND

...a man is a slave to whatever has mastered him.

2 PETER 2:19 NIV

When I was a young girl I was constantly on one crazy diet after another. I can tell you from experience, all they do is mess up your metabolism. Your body doesn't know whether to go ahead and burn up what you give it or try to hang on to it because it may not get anything else for a week or more.

If you have been starving your body for a month, not allowing it any carbohydrates, for example, and you suddenly change diets and give it a dose of carbohydrates, your body won't know what to do. It will probably say, "I'm going to hold on to this because I may never get any more."

When women get pregnant they usually start to gain weight, so as soon as the baby is born they go on some kind of weird diet. From then on, for the rest of their lives, they can never maintain a normal, sensible weight simply because their metabolism may be so "out of whack." It wasn't having the baby that caused problems with their metabolism, it was the crazy things they did trying to get back to the same dress size they wore before they got pregnant.

"But what am I supposed to do?" you may ask.

You are supposed to do normal things. You are supposed to eat balanced meals. You are supposed to eat a little bit of everything you need without overdoing it. You are supposed to exercise enough to burn off what you eat so it doesn't just stay on you.

Don't get trapped on the diet-go-round. I hope you won't feel like stoning me when I say this, but I think if you have to be on a diet all your life you are in bondage.

Now you may get on some healthy eating program and start learning good eating habits. I am not opposed to that at all. But if you have to go around with food on your mind all the time, counting everything you put in your mouth, and worrying about everything you eat, that is bondage.

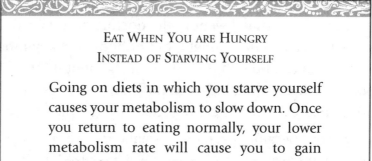

EAT WHEN YOU ARE HUNGRY
INSTEAD OF STARVING YOURSELF

Going on diets in which you starve yourself causes your metabolism to slow down. Once you return to eating normally, your lower metabolism rate will cause you to gain weight faster than before you fasted. The next time you diet by starving yourself, your metabolism will drop even more quickly and lower, causing you to have an even more difficult time losing weight.[1]

THE BONDAGE OF DIETS

So if the Son liberates you [makes you free men], then you
are really and unquestionably free.

JOHN 8:36

When I became pregnant with my first child, I was
in my early twenties. I really didn't know how to care
for myself properly. I was going through a clinic, and I
had a different doctor every time I went. I wasn't getting
any kind of teaching, and I didn't understand anything
about being pregnant or delivering a baby. I didn't
understand anything about how you ought to eat. I was
just about as ignorant about having a baby as anybody
could be.

I was very upset because the man I was married to
had left me and was living with another woman. I was
so upset I wasn't eating. I was actually losing weight all
the time. Every time I went to the doctor and weighed, I
knew I wasn't gaining weight, but nobody said anything
to me about it. I didn't think too much about it. And
because I was getting bigger as the baby grew, I didn't
notice really that I was getting smaller other places.

When I became pregnant, I weighed 153 pounds,
and when I went in for delivery I weighed 153½! While
I was pregnant, I lost eighteen or twenty pounds. The
minute I delivered the baby, of course, my stomach
went down. After two or three days in the hospital, I
came out of the hospital weighing less than I had ever
weighed in my adult life: 135 pounds!

I was ecstatic! I thought I was the greatest looking thing that had hit St. Louis for a while! I was so excited about the way that I looked. I had never felt so good about myself because I had never been little. It was great fun, but the problem was I went into even a worse bondage than of trying to lose weight — the bondage of being on diets.

Up until that time, I had never dieted. I had always known I was overweight, but I knew nothing about calories or anything else related to proper nutrition. Because I knew nothing about weight control, I didn't bother with it. I just ate and stayed overweight because I didn't know what to do about my condition.

After I lost that weight and liked it so much, I decided I was never going to be overweight again — and I have a strong will. The only problem with my decision was that it led me into the bondage of diets.

If you have never had an eating problem, you may not fully understand what I am referring to by that term. But the truth is, it doesn't matter how thin you and I are, if we have food on our mind all the time, we are in bondage just as much as if we have to count every calorie that goes into our mouths.

The real issue is not thin versus fat, it is bondage versus freedom. God does not want His children to be in bondage to anything. That's why He sent Jesus to set us free, and the *King James Version* of John 8:36 says that whom the Son sets free is free indeed.

My purpose in writing this book is to share with you how to be set free from the bondage of diets — and there are lots them! I know, because at one time or another I tried them *all*.

I tried low-calorie diets, low-carbohydrate diets, and low-fat diets. I tried liquid diets, including some kind of powered stuff that went into me and acted like brick mortar. I thought I was going to die before I finally got it flushed out of my system.

I tried grapefruit diets. I was told if I ate a grapefruit or drank grapefruit juice before every meal it would burn up the calories. I had so much grapefruit juice in my stomach, it filled with acid and caused my face to break out in pimples.

I tried a hard-boiled egg diet. I tried a banana and milk diet. I tried low-protein diets and high-protein diets.

Then someone told me about the mixed food diet. Supposedly if I mixed the right food groups together my body would burn off the calories. Of course, like all the rest of these diets, it didn't work — at least not for me. All it did was keep my mind constantly on food.

GET YOUR MIND OFF FOOD

> For all who are led by the Spirit of God are sons of God.
>
> ROMANS 8:14

As Christians, we are to be free to be led by the Spirit, not by the latest fad diet. We need to get enough information from God to know what to eat and what not to eat, when to eat and when not to eat, when to say yes to food, and when to say no.

When I first got serious about maintaining a proper eating and weight program, I read books and books on the subject. It was amazing to me how much it helped me to be educated, to be informed about things like nutrition. I learned what foods had what vitamins in them and how much protein I needed every day and how important it is to drink water and how vital exercise is to proper health.

Many times when we Christians have problems, we start looking for some devil to blame. Often our problems are not caused by the devil but by our own ignorance. That's why we need to get educated and stay informed about food and proper nutrition.

Every once in a while I will get lax in some area and start feeling bad because I know I am not eating properly. I may put on a few pounds because I am not applying what I know about food. When I start to fall back into my old habits I will get out a good book on nutrition and start rereading it. Just as we turn to the Bible when we start getting into trouble with anger or some other harmful emotion, so we have to return to what we know about proper eating habits.

STAY EDUCATED AND STAY CONFIDENT

So do not throw away your confidence; it will be richly rewarded.

HEBREWS 10:35 NIV

A young lady who works in our ministry has a bit of a weight problem. She told me recently how much it has helped her to get educated by reading books on nutrition.

"I have to do that every once in a while just to keep sharp in certain areas," she said. "It gives me confidence when I read those books. It motivates me and strengthens me to do the right thing."

That's true. That's why we all need to get educated and stay educated, because we have to be on our guard all the time to resist temptation.

For example, many times I have gone to the grocery store and purchased fruit and cottage cheese and yogurt when I knew I was going out with my family to a fast-food hamburger place.

We have to be familiar enough with ourselves to know what we can do and what we cannot do. I know what I can do to stay the same weight, and I know what happens to me if I don't stick to what I know. If I allow myself to get very far off my eating and exercise program, I begin to come under condemnation. I don't like the way I look and feel, which as I have said, affects my sense of confidence, which in turn affects my ministry.

I can't stand up in front of people and minister in confidence if I have something else on my mind all the time. I can't meditate on the Word of God if I am meditating on food or my feelings or my appearance. I can't hear from God if all I am listening to is my own mind and body.

That's why I believe food is a much greater problem for us believers than most of us realize. It robs us of our inheritance of peace, joy, and harmony.

GET ALONG WITH YOURSELF AND OTHERS

...let's agree to use all our energy in getting along with each other.

ROMANS 14:16 MESSAGE

When people are fighting a weight or eating problem, when they have food on their mind all the time, often it makes them cranky and grouchy.

The young woman in our ministry who has a slight weight problem has said that she is much friendlier, sweeter, and easier to get along with when she doesn't have her mind on food all the time. That's true of all of us. We act better when we feel better, and we feel better when we know we are in control of our own lives. We don't like to feel that we are being controlled by other people or things — like food — which is a form of bondage.

When we eat and exercise properly, we just feel better about ourselves. And the better we feel about ourselves, the easier we are to get along with.

Years ago I discovered if I don't like myself I am not going to get along with anybody else. That was a great revelation to me. It was enough to teach me to do whatever I had to do to keep myself in shape, even if it seemed radical to other people.

GET RADICAL, IF NECESSARY

If the way you live isn't consistent with what you believe, then it's wrong.

ROMANS 14:23 MESSAGE

As I have noted, many times when I am out with my family and we get hungry, there is no time to look all over for some place that serves the kind of food I need. In that case, I just stop at a grocery store and buy some fruit, cottage cheese, and yogurt and take it with me to the fast-food restaurant. My family eats what they want, and I eat what I want.

You may think, "That's pretty radical."

It may be radical, and it may take a bit of extra effort, but it works. I know it works because I am not overweight and unhappy anymore. And that's the bottom line.

Sometimes if you want to get the right results, you have to take some radical steps.

Another young lady in our ministry feels really strong about being healthy and eating wisely, so she carries all kinds of health food with her when we are on the road. Everybody teases her and says she carries a bag of birdseed because she is always nibbling on sunflower seeds. She doesn't mind being teased because she knows what's good for her.

For years she was very sick until God showed her that she could be healthy if she would put the right things into her body and take care of herself. She is not going to throw away what God has told her, so she goes to the extreme of taking with her what she needs. That may sound radical to some people, but not to her because she is educated. She knows what works for her and what doesn't, and she sticks to it regardless of what other people think or say. That's the way we all should be.

THE IMPORTANCE OF WATER

...give me also springs of water....

JUDGES 1:15

One of the right things we are to put into our bodies is water. Without it our system will not work as it was designed to function.

What did God put on earth for us to drink? Water. What do human beings need for their bodies to function properly? Water. How many calories does water have? None.

Isn't it amazing that God had all that figured out? Our trouble is, we take the basic ingredient He provided and mix into it all kinds of herbs and chemicals and sugar and then wonder why we don't feel good or why we gain weight.

Most health experts agree that the human body needs eight glasses of water a day. Water suppresses the appetite naturally and helps the body metabolize stored fat. Oddly enough, drinking plenty of water is the best treatment for fluid retention. So those of us who have trouble because our bodies hold water need to drink more water, not less.

Water helps to maintain proper muscle tone. It helps rid the body of waste and other impurities. It can also help relieve constipation.

All these facts are good reasons for drinking lots of water, which is so essential to the proper functioning of the human body.

Some people claim they do not like water or they have an intolerance to it. But I believe if God put it here for our use and made our bodies so dependent upon it, He must have had a good reason for doing so. We need to quit making excuses and start doing what He has showed us to be His way of maintaining proper weight and good health.

When I am on the road ministering, I usually carry two things with me: a gold water bottle holder and a silver one! I got them to match my outfits. I have learned that it is possible to be both fashionable and healthy. I get a lot of comments about my water bottle holders. Many people say, "That's a good idea!"

I have even been teased about going into the "Life in the Word Water Bottle Business" — because I know how important water is to good health. I have found that it helps wash toxins out of the body, improves bladder and bowel function, curbs appetite, and so much more.

I have also discovered that the only way I can be sure of having enough water to drink is by taking it along with me wherever I go. In addition, I have discovered that room temperature water is easier to drink than ice cold water, so I can drink more of it.

Go to the extreme of carrying drinking water with you. Buy a water jug and keep it in the car. Buy a smaller bottle to carry in your purse or on your belt when you go places like shopping or walking.

Plan Ahead

> Any enterprise is built by wise planning....
>
> Proverbs 24:3 tlb

When I travel, I also carry along an "in-case" package. There are times when I have to rush to catch a plane so I don't have time to eat. If I don't provide something for myself I will end up eating what is served on the plane — peanuts, pretzels, and soda pop — none of which I need. Although I am hungry, instead of consuming all that salt, fat, and calories, I usually wait till I get home and sit down and have a nice meal.

To handle situations like that I have learned to plan ahead. I carry a little bag of goodies with me. I may have a couple of apples for me and Dave (because I know if he sees me eating one, he will want one too). I may have some vitamins and, just in case I get too hungry, some little health bars that taste almost like a candy bar but are chock full of nutrition.

That's just one way to fight the devil and avoid temptation — by planning ahead. The other is by exercising restraint.

EXERCISE RESTRAINT

> For the grace of God that brings salvation has appeared to all men. It teaches us to say "No" to ungodliness and worldly passions, and to live self-controlled, upright and godly lives....
>
> TITUS 2:11,12 NIV

If we are going to walk in victory in this area, we are not going to get everything we like or want. We are going to have to learn to say no every single solitary day of our lives — and more than once a day.

When I was young I was always chunky and always on a diet. But no matter how many different diets I tried, they never worked. I would lose weight for a while, but then I would gain it all back again. That went on until I became educated about proper diet and nutrition and exercise.

If you are struggling with an eating or weight problem, you need to get educated. You need to know yourself and your body and how it functions. You need to know how many calories and grams of fat your body can handle and what to do to keep within those limits.

That doesn't mean you have to go around with a calculator and a sheet of paper in your hands for the rest of your life. Once you know what you can and can't handle, it will become almost automatic. Although you may have to carry a calculator and a piece of paper for a time, after a while you will know when and what you can eat and how much. That way you can plan your eating and keep your weight under control.

It is not a question of depriving yourself. It is a matter of exercising a little bit of restraint. If you will do that, I believe with all my heart that the Holy Spirit will lead you and help you maintain a balanced diet so you can live in health and joy.

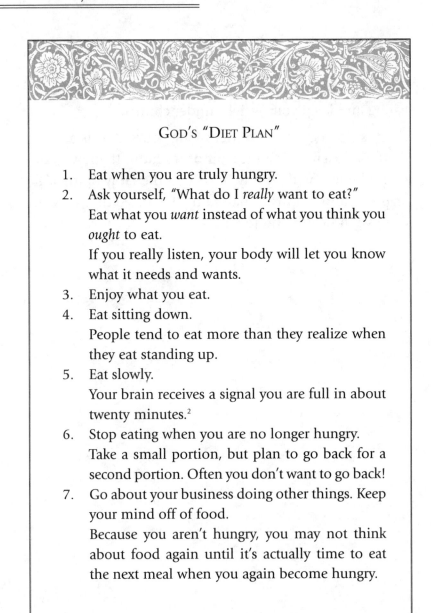

GOD'S "DIET PLAN"

1. Eat when you are truly hungry.
2. Ask yourself, "What do I *really* want to eat?"
   Eat what you *want* instead of what you think you *ought* to eat.
   If you really listen, your body will let you know what it needs and wants.
3. Enjoy what you eat.
4. Eat sitting down.
   People tend to eat more than they realize when they eat standing up.
5. Eat slowly.
   Your brain receives a signal you are full in about twenty minutes.[2]
6. Stop eating when you are no longer hungry.
   Take a small portion, but plan to go back for a second portion. Often you don't want to go back!
7. Go about your business doing other things. Keep your mind off of food.
   Because you aren't hungry, you may not think about food again until it's actually time to eat the next meal when you again become hungry.

8. Enjoy other things besides eating.

   There's not a thing wrong with going out to eat as entertainment as long as it is *one* of your forms of entertainment. Increase your enjoyment of your other interests.

9. Follow the leading of the Holy Spirit.

   He will tell you what is right for you and lead you into victory and freedom, not into gaining weight!

10. Step out in faith to obey the leading of the Holy Spirit.

   If He leads you one day to eat a bowl of cereal for breakfast instead of half a grapefruit and toast, or an occasional small piece of pie after a satisfying dinner, do it. (If you feel deprived from never eating a piece of pie, you may be tempted to eat half a pie at some point!)

Reason 2:

Lack of a Balanced Diet

Reason 2:

Lack of a Balanced Diet

*Be well balanced (temperate,
sober of mind), be vigilant and cautious
at all times; for that enemy of yours,
the devil, roams around like a lion
roaring [in fierce hunger], seeking
someone to seize upon and devour.*

1 PETER 5:8

The problem with many people's diet is that it is unbalanced. They eat too much starch and not enough protein, or too much protein and not enough carbohydrates. They may follow one of those diets that say, "Eat all of this and none of that."

If God had wanted us to eat just one food or kind of foods, He would not have created the abundance and variety of good things that are available to us.

The Bible teaches us that we are to be balanced in every area of our lives, including eating. Just as it is balanced living that brings victory, it is balanced eating that brings health.

That does not mean that we should all eat the same things at the same time or in the same amounts. Each person's diet should be uniquely suited to that individual's needs.

I need a lot of protein in my diet. Over the years I have tried many diets that limit protein, and I have always ended up wanting something all the time. If I eat plenty of protein, I may not feel full all the time, but I do feel satisfied.

I have also learned that I need a lot of water. Sometimes when I get hungry before mealtime, a full glass of water will take the edge off my appetite. As we have seen, water is an important part of any well-balanced diet.

If you are going to follow a balanced diet, don't eat the same thing all the time. Rotate your food. It helps provide variety, which increases your sense of satisfaction.

This is a problem for me because if I find I like something, I want to eat it every day. If I do that, I will eventually get so fed up with it that I never want to eat it again as long as I live. That is not eating in moderation.

ALL THINGS IN MODERATION

Let your moderation be known unto all men....

PHILIPPIANS 4:5 KJV

Some people become unable to tolerate their favorite foods. One reason they can no longer tolerate them is that they eat them so much their body begins to reject them.

If they go to an allergist, the first thing he will do is put them on a rotation diet so their body can adapt to a balanced diet. All this is part of the balanced life that God wants us to live.

The Bible teaches that we are to do all things in moderation. To be moderate is to be temperate or balanced. To be balanced is to be regular.

Do you ever try to see how long you can go without eating, thinking that skipping meals is going to make you lose weight? Often it only makes you hungrier so that when you do eat, you gobble up everything in sight. Then you think, "I don't know why I'm so overweight, I go all day without eating."

I used to do that all the time. For years and years I was caught in that trap. I would never eat until three or four o'clock in the afternoon. I would spend most of the day smoking cigarettes and drinking coffee, then I would spend the rest of the day and night eating. I couldn't figure out why I never lost any weight.

One young lady used to complain that she couldn't understand why she was so overweight. "I never eat," she said.

"Yes, you do," her husband said. "You eat bread all the time."

This woman loved bread, so she ate it constantly. But to her way of thinking she was not eating anything at all. She was eating, but not in a balanced way. As a result she was always hungry and always overweight.

Like so many of us, this young woman was deceived.

DO NOT BE DECEIVED

Do not be deceived....A man reaps what he sows.

GALATIANS 6:7 NIV

Often we think, "I'm not eating anything." But we usually are eating something, just not the right things or the right amount.

If you don't eat the right things, but you do eat the wrong things, even though you are eating only a little bit of the wrong things, you would be better off eating a lot of the right things.

It is amazing how many nutritious foods like fruits and vegetables you can eat and not gain any weight, and maybe even lose weight. At the same time, it is amazing how little junk food like candy or potato chips you can eat and still gain weight.

So the question is not just how much food you eat, it is also what kind of food you eat and when you eat it.

GETTING BACK INTO BALANCE

Keep watch over yourselves....

ACTS 20:28 NIV

If you have been eating the wrong kinds and amounts of foods, your system may be out of balance. Here's how to get it back in balance: *Stop going on fad diets.*

Stop trying to lose weight by following some prescribed or self-imposed diet plan. Instead, go on a good, quality eating program. Begin by listening to your body.

When I say to listen to your body, please understand I am not talking about your *carnal* nature, the sinful, unhealthy cravings that lead to misery and destruction. I am talking about the sensible, healthy hungers that need to be satisfied in order to keep the body working the way God intended.

EAT MORE TO LOSE WEIGHT

One of the best ways of losing weight may be to eat more of certain foods! Low-fat foods which are high in fiber (such as popcorn) contain fewer calories than high-fat foods (such as peanuts), and fat has more than twice as many calories as carbohydrates or proteins. You could eat much more popcorn containing 150 calories than you could of peanuts with the same number of calories!

If you will listen to your body carefully and wisely, it will tell you what it needs to maintain proper balance so it can serve you as it should.

Remember, your body was designed to be your servant, you are not to serve it. When it wears out, you are going to be in trouble. So learn to respect it and take care of it. Listen to the messages it sends you about what it needs — proper diet, exercise, rest, sleep, recreation — in order to keep itself in prime working condition.

EAT RIGHT AND LIVE LONG

Go your way, eat your bread with joy, and drink your wine
with a cheerful heart [if you are righteous, wise, and in the
hands of God], for God has already accepted your works.

ECCLESIASTES 9:7

Everything I have read and seen lately has confirmed
what I believe God has shown me over the years: If you
and I will eat the right foods in the right amount,
sooner or later our bodies will settle down to the weight
that is best for us individually.

That does not necessarily mean if you start eating
properly today you will lose weight tomorrow. You may
start losing weight in two weeks or in three months. You
may go for six months and not lose a single pound. In
fact, you may actually gain weight for a while, especially
if you have just come off a crash diet in which you lost
weight by starving — because you lost those pounds
unfairly, so to speak.

Your body will need time to adjust to your new
wholesome way of eating and exercising. Once it regains
its proper balance, you will slowly but steadily start
losing weight, usually about two to six pounds a month.

You may be thinking, "There is no way I am going
to wait six months to start losing a couple of pounds
a month!"

Isn't that better than spending the next six months
losing and gaining the same ten pounds over and over

again? That is as unhealthy as it is unwise. God's way of sensible eating and exercise is much better — and much longer lasting.

IT'S JUST A MATTER OF TIME

He has made everything beautiful in its time....

ECCLESIASTES 3:11

If you have abused your body for a long period, you will have to treat it right for a while before it will start working right for you.

When a couple in a marriage relationship mistreat one another for years, even though they may finally reconcile there will still be a period of adjustment to be gone through. The memory of their past hurts will not disappear overnight. It takes time to restore lost faith and trust.

The same is true in the relationship between you and your body. If you have abused it for a long time by feast and famine, bingeing and purging, lavish meals one day and two diet pills the next, it may not know what to expect from you anymore. It may have temporarily lost its ability to establish and maintain a proper balance. But if you will stick to a sensible eating and exercise program, sooner or later your body will stabilize and will begin to serve you properly once again.

It's just a matter of time.

Anything You Want — Within Reason

But solid food is for full-grown men, for those whose
senses and mental faculties are trained by practice to discrimi-
nate and distinguish between what is...good and...what is...con-
trary either to divine or human law.

HEBREWS 5:14

I once talked to a young woman in Chicago who
said she had been sixty-five pounds overweight and had
become sick and had to go on a sensible, high-quality
eating program of almost all natural foods: good lean
meat, lots of fruits and vegetables, plenty of liquids,
especially water — and moderate exercise.

She said after two weeks she started to lose weight.
She lost so much, in fact, she had to try to gain back
seven pounds.

"Apparently," she told me, "I have got my system
normalized. Now I eat anything I want, within reason,
and I never gain an ounce."

Notice that phrase "within reason."

The problem with many overweight people is they
go on a diet to hurry up and lose weight so they can get
back to eating anything they want — which puts the
weight right back on, so the whole process has to begin
again. That is the classic feast and famine cycle which is
so dangerous and unhealthy.

This young woman said now that she has her system
normalized she can eat anything she wants — *within reason.*

That is the key.

Yes, you and I can get to the place of eating anything we want to — as long as we get our "want-to" straightened out.

This young woman was not talking about eating all the junk food she wanted. Instead, she was talking about eating all she wanted of the right foods her body called for.

On God's eating program, we can eat anything we want, as long as we have the wisdom to know what to want.

WHAT DO YOU *REALLY WANT* TO EAT?

Sometimes your soul and flesh
make ridiculous demands on you.

Do you really want a hot fudge sundae for breakfast?

When you stop to figure out if you really want something like this, ninety-nine and nine-tenths of the time you will find out you really don't. But maybe some other time, in the evening after dinner, you think about it again and decide you really do want a hot fudge sundae! Go ahead and eat it. It is continual excess that causes trouble — not occasional liberties.

God created a wide variety of foods for us to eat. Every good food God made, you can eat.

Take the time to learn how to get in touch with what you really want to eat.

NOT A DIET BUT A LIFESTYLE

...Such is your own verdict; you yourself have decided it.

1 KINGS 20:40

What God is offering us is not a diet but a lifestyle. *The solution to being overweight is not a temporary deprivation, it is a permanent decision.*

One reason I have not gained any significant weight for years now is that I made a permanent decision to change — not my diet, but my lifestyle. I came to that decision when God showed me diets are not the answer because they simply do not work, at least not for long.

If you and I are really serious about reaching our proper weight and maintaining it for the rest of our life, if we want to stay strong and healthy until our Lord comes for us, we must learn to eat the right foods in the right amounts — as long as we live.

The answer to an eating or weight problem is a balanced diet made up of a variety of wholesome, nutritious foods eaten at the right times and in the right amounts.

Reason 3:

Lack of Exercise

Reason 3:
Lack of Exercise

Exercise daily in God — no
...flabbiness, please!

1 TIMOTHY 4:7 MESSAGE

The reason most people are overweight is very simple: they take in more calories than they burn up. There's nothing else to be said. That's about all anyone really needs to know about the subject.

That's why we cannot expect to lose weight if we don't change our eating and exercise habits, especially as we get older and begin to do less physically.

A young man may play a lot of sports and stay slim and healthy. Then he gets married, settles down, and has two or three children. Now instead of spending all his free time playing sports, when he is not at work he is at home sitting in front of the television. Yet he keeps eating the same way he did when he was physically active. It's no wonder that sooner or later he begins to put on weight — just because of the change in his lifestyle.

EXERCISE MAKES A DIFFERENCE

Workouts in the gymnasium are useful....

1 TIMOTHY 4:8 MESSAGE

When my husband and I got married, he was not overweight at all. When he reached about forty years of age he decided he was getting a little bit chunkier than he wanted to be. Suddenly I noticed that he wasn't eating dinner.

"Why aren't you eating dinner?" I asked him.

"Because I want to lose some weight," he said. "Something has changed in my body, and I just can't eat as much as I used to without putting on weight. When I was in the army and playing basketball regularly, I could pile up my plate with food and eat and eat. Now that I'm not exercising as much, I can't do that anymore."

He went without eating dinner for about two weeks and lost fifteen pounds and has never gained it back. After that he either had to reduce his eating or increase his exercise in order to maintain the weight he felt was best for him.

That is true for all of us. Either we change our eating and exercise habits as our lifestyle changes, or we end up gaining weight. That's just the way it works.

EXERCISE IS MOVEMENT

> For in Him we live and *move* and have our being...For we are also His offspring.
>
> ACTS 17:28

The exercise I am talking about is really just movement. Americans today don't move enough. We sit too much. We ride everywhere we go. We think we are working hard when we push buttons:

"Who says I don't work! Why, I did the dishes (in the automatic dishwasher). I did four loads of laundry (in the automatic washer-dryer). I directed the housekeeper (who did all the real work)."

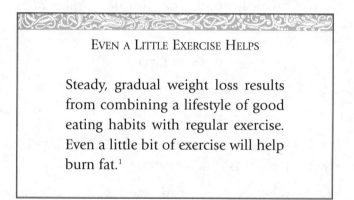

EVEN A LITTLE EXERCISE HELPS

Steady, gradual weight loss results from combining a lifestyle of good eating habits with regular exercise. Even a little bit of exercise will help burn fat.[1]

We don't even know what real work is, as compared to a hundred years ago when people had to do almost everything by hand.

I will be honest with you. I think Satan has put one over on us. He has made everything so easy and comfortable and convenient that it is killing us. We don't have to walk up steps because there are elevators and escalators. We don't have to cook because everything is instant and "microwaveable." We don't have to push a lawn mower because we either have a riding mower or we hire the job done. We don't have to lift or carry or clean because there is someone there to do it for us. We don't even have to get out of the car when we go shopping because everything is drive-through.

We fall for the devil's deception. We think we are saving time and effort, but we are really losing strength and energy — and gaining stress and frustration. We drive through life until we break down, then we want a breakthrough. The trouble is, *there are no drive-through breakthroughs.*

IT TAKES EFFORT

And herein do I exercise myself....

ACTS 24:16 KJV

It takes effort to lose weight and keep it off permanently. That effort is called exercise.

I know whenever the word "exercise" is mentioned, everybody groans even thinking about it. I feel exactly the same way. Believe me, I don't like it any more than anybody else does. But the bottom line is, we have to get some movement in our bodies if we ever expect to lose weight and feel good about ourselves.

I know it's hard to work sensible exercise into our daily life. If we go on using elevators, escalators, riding mowers, automatic dishwashers and washer-dryers, and automobiles, we will never get the type or the amount of exercise we need. That means we are going to have to make a conscious effort to avoid some of these modern "labor-saving devices."

For example, instead of driving everywhere you go, try walking some place once in a while. It won't be the end of the world. Instead of taking the elevator or escalator, try climbing the stairs. Instead of using a riding lawn mower or hiring your grass cut, try mowing it yourself. Sure, it may cause you to work up a sweat, but that's the whole point.

In our climate-controlled society we go from air-conditioned car to air-conditioned building and back again. Because we never really sweat, we never wash the toxins out of our bodies. Then we wonder why we feel bad all the time.

It is unwise to seek a life of luxury that requires no effort on our part. If the only exercise we get is mowing the lawn once a week, then we need to think twice before buying a self-propelled or riding lawn mower. The world will tell us that we don't need to be out mowing and working up a sweat, but just the opposite could be true. We may need that bit of exercise because it could be the only thing that is keeping us as healthy as we are.

The same is true of any other so-called labor-saving device or appliance.

We have made everything in life so easy, so convenient, so effortless, that we are killing ourselves for lack of exercise.

The unending search for ease and convenience is a sign of laziness. I believe there is a lazy spirit at loose in our society today — even in our churches. We don't even want to sit in church any more unless we have a padded seat. We don't want to have to walk across the parking lot, and we sure won't stay if the church building isn't air-conditioned. We have become too lazy for our own good.

EXERCISE ON PURPOSE

...exercise thyself....

1 TIMOTHY 4:7 KJV

Because our lifestyles don't provide much exercise, we must exercise on purpose. Since exercise is defined simply as movement, any movement will help.

When I am working at my computer all day, every so often I will get up and take a break. I have an exercise ball that I use to relieve tension and fatigue. It was given to me by my chiropractor. Many times I will just go in and sit on that ball for five minutes, or I may bounce around on it for a while. Anything that keeps the body moving — even stretching, even laughing — starts the blood to flowing, which is good.

The bottom line is, when it comes to exercise, do whatever works for you.

I have to admit that I can't do floor exercises. They just don't work for me. I can only work out on a treadmill if I am doing something constructive like discussing business with my secretary at the same time. I have to have something to take my mind off the treadmill. I just can't stand there for forty-five minutes doing nothing but walking. It seems like such a waste of time to me. I need to feel like I am accomplishing something with my time.

Two things I have discovered that relax me and take my mind off my work are playing golf and walking. I like to play golf with my husband Dave. I get good exercise, and I enjoy walking. I try to walk several miles a week, two or three miles at a time, three or four times weekly.

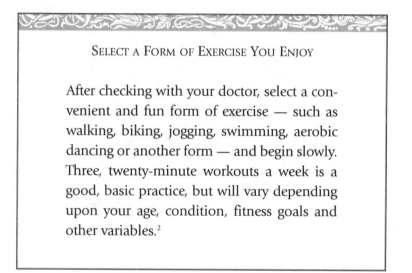

SELECT A FORM OF EXERCISE YOU ENJOY

After checking with your doctor, select a convenient and fun form of exercise — such as walking, biking, jogging, swimming, aerobic dancing or another form — and begin slowly. Three, twenty-minute workouts a week is a good, basic practice, but will vary depending upon your age, condition, fitness goals and other variables.[2]

You have to find out what is best for you. If you enjoy being with other people while you exercise, you may want to belong to a gym or join a health center. If you can exercise at home alone, then you may be able to get down on the floor and follow a television fitness program or work along with an exercise video.

The main thing is, whatever it takes to get your body in motion, your muscles working, and your blood flowing, do it! Get moving!

Reason 4:

Bad Eating Habits

Reason 4:

Bad Eating Habits

*...Eat only as much as is sufficient
for you, lest, being filled with it,
you vomit it.*

PROVERBS 25:16

*P*ossibly the number one reason people have problems with their weight is simply bad eating habits.

We will look at some of these habits to see what can be done to overcome them.

1. Eating just before going to bed.

I have done that all my life, and it is a bad habit. I still do it, but at least now I am very careful about what I eat. I usually try to stick with fruit or some other non-fattening food that is good for me.

I heard of one lady who said that for years she drank a glass of milk every night before she went to bed. By just breaking that habit she lost twelve pounds in a year.

2. Wanting to feel full all the time.

A young lady once read a book which said, "If you want to be thin, go interview some thin people and find out how they eat."

So she went and talked to another young woman who was so thin she wore a size six dress.

"I want to lose weight," she said. "Tell me about your eating habits. How often do you think about food?"

"Well," answered the thin woman, "I don't think about food at all unless I get hungry."

That is an important point. Most people who are overweight think about food all the time.

"When do you stop eating?" she was asked.

"Oh, I stop eating," she answered, "as soon as I feel just comfortable."

That is another important point. Most overweight people eat until they are stuffed. In fact, most often they don't feel like they have eaten unless they are so full they can hardly breathe.

If you are having an eating or weight problem, try to develop the habit of eating only when you are really hungry, and then stopping when you feel comfortably full, not stuffed.

This young woman went on to say, "I don't eat until my stomach starts growling."

"How long is that?" she was asked. "How long do you usually go between meals?"

"Well, the first time I did it," she answered, "it took me two and a half days to get really hungry."

She must have built up a lot of reserve to go that long without getting really hungry! You and I probably won't be able to go that long before we start feeling hunger pangs. But even then we need to use restraint when we start eating so we don't go to excess and stuff ourselves.

It is possible to get to the point where you absolutely hate the feeling of being stuffed. When you have reached that point, you are well on your way to maintaining proper weight.

3. *Having to have something sweet after every meal.*

Feeling that we must have at least one bite of something sweet after every meal is simply a habit, and it is one we should all try to break, if we have it. I can break this habit and be free for a long time then get back into it again. As I listen to people, it is amazing how many say after eating, "I just want a bite of something sweet." How could one bite of something possibly satisfy our bodies? It must be a mental habit — we think we have to have something.

When Dave and I are eating out, I am always trying to push him to order dessert for himself so I can snitch a couple of bites for myself. I think he has finally figured out my strategy. He realizes that he would have some major health problems if he ate everything I try to get him to order just so I can sneak some of it.

Eating sweets after every meal, or even every day, is a bad habit we all need to break.

4. *Snacking while watching television or movies.*

If you have this habit and feel that you just have to have something to munch on while you watch TV, try snacking on something healthy. You may not like this suggestion, but try nibbling on carrot sticks instead of potato chips.

When you go to the movies, instead of eating popcorn, candy, or drinking soda pop, take your own healthy snacks along with you.

Get out of the habit of always having to have some rich, fattening snack every time you sit down for a bit of entertainment. If I am going out in the evening to a place where I want to enjoy some food I normally do not eat, I plan ahead for it. For example, if I am going to the movies and I have decided I really want to eat popcorn at the movie (with a little butter), I leave some-thing else out of my diet that day to make up for the extra calories I will consume in the evening. As I said previously, it is not the "occasional liberties" that cause trouble. The key to victory is to make sure they are "occasional," and that they don't become a daily habit that controls us.

5. *Eating just because others are eating, because food is available or advertised, or because of anger or upset.*

These points will be discussed in more detail later on. But for now don't feel that you have to eat every time you get around people who are eating or every time you come into contact with food or snacks.

Don't feel that you have to get up and go to the kitchen and fix a snack or go out to the store and buy some food product just because it is shown on television or pictured in a magazine.

Finally, don't feel that you have eat to find comfort in food when you get emotional or to spite someone who has offended you. You are not hurting anybody but yourself.

Someone has said that it takes thirty days to make or break a habit. Get some new habits. Keep some low-calorie, low-fat, low-cholesterol snacks around the house or office or in your car so when you want a bite to eat between meals you can reach for something that is not going to put a lot of weight on you.

Break your bad-eating habits with good habits like taking a walk every day. You will look better and feel better.

Reason 5:

Unbalanced Metabolism

Reason 5:
Unbalanced Metabolism

One...may eat anything, while a weaker one [limits his] eating to vegetables.

ROMANS 14:2

*A*n unbalanced metabolism is one of the reasons why some people are overweight. Wouldn't we all like to believe that is our problem?

"I just can't help being overweight," we moan pitifully, "my metabolism is out of balance; it's my hormones!"

Today it seems that everything gets blamed on metabolism or hormones. When the doctor can't find anything else to explain our condition, we can always blame our metabolism or lay it off on our hormones.

We like that situation because it relieves us of our responsibility to do something about ourselves. After all, if our metabolism or our hormones are "out of whack," there is nothing we can do about it.

That is not entirely true.

Remove far from me vanity and lies:...feed me with food convenient for me.

PROVERBS 30:8 KJV

Metabolism is simply the rate at which the body burns food and turns it into energy for use. Interestingly enough, there are two things that affect metabolism: 1) exercise, and 2) eating. The first, exercise, is simple: the more a person exercises, the faster his metabolism rate. The other, eating, is even more interesting.

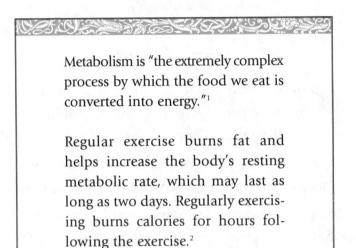

Metabolism is "the extremely complex process by which the food we eat is converted into energy."[1]

Regular exercise burns fat and helps increase the body's resting metabolic rate, which may last as long as two days. Regularly exercising burns calories for hours following the exercise.[2]

Recently I read some very informative material on the hypothalamus, the portion of the brain that regulates metabolism of fats and carbohydrates.[3]

One way the body maintains a set point is by releasing a protein made by fat cells into the bloodstream. Its release signals the brain that fat cells are "full," (in other words, the body has reached its set point) and produces a reduction in eating. Another way is through an enzyme manufactured by fat cells that removes fat recently eaten from the bloodstream. The enzyme can become very active in order to increase the efficiency of the body's fat storage and maintain the set point when fat and calories are reduced.

The problem is that when we go on and off diets, we are actually working against our bodies in our attempts to lose weight. Our bodies respond to the state of starvation or semi-starvation brought on by the diets with a fight to maintain the set point rather than lower it. As we saw before, starving ourselves causes our metabolism to slow down.

To keep our metabolism working properly so that our bodies will lose weight and reach the set point that will carry the amount of weight for which they were designed, we must establish a good eating program and maintain it for an extended time.[4]

If you are like me, you have been on so many diets over the years you have lost and then gained back a thousand pounds. The reason we keep losing and gaining is that we have not been cooperating with our body's individual set point for our ideal weight.

The answer is not a new diet of some kind. The answer is the original plan of God, which is for us to eat the foods He has created for us in the amounts He intends for us to have.

In the form of the hypothalamus, God has placed within each of us a tiny "computer" programmed to monitor our eating habits and inform us what to eat and when to eat it.

Many people are in poor health simply because they do not eat the right kinds of food for them. They go on fad diets that eliminate some of the basic food groups, which is very detrimental to health. Many even end up in hospitals because they deprive their bodies for such long periods of time of the essential vitamins, minerals, and other nutrients necessary for proper physical and mental health.

It is especially important for women to eat the right foods in the right amount while they are young in preparation for that time later on called "the change of life." If a woman's body is not nutritionally sound, when she reaches a certain age, she can end up in serious trouble. The problem is that often women are more sensitive of their weight and shape than men are, which can lead them to abuse or neglect their health.

One time I went on a fast and lost a lot of weight. Then vanity took over. A wealthy person had given me some very expensive clothes, all size four, and I wanted to be able to keep wearing them. So I spent the next three months living on soup, lettuce, and fruit, eating only one small meal a day. My body became so run down the devil used that opportunity to attack me at a time when I was not physically able to resist him. As a result, I began to experience all kinds of disturbing symptoms.

Even though we Christians have authority over the devil and are empowered to resist and overcome his attacks, we still have to take care of ourselves. God cannot bless us if we are abusing our bodies for the sake of vanity.

When I realized what I was doing, I repented and asked the Lord to help me get back on a healthy eating program that was right for me.

That is as important for men as it is for women. Just as women must go through the change of life, men often have to face mid-life crises. They need to be in good mental and physical condition in order to withstand the stresses and pressures that can come during those trying times.

Set a Standard and Keep To It

...Hearken diligently to Me, and eat what is good....

Isaiah 55:2

I happen to have a slower rate of metabolism than many of the people with whom I come into contact on a daily basis. It has been that way all of my life. When I was a teenager I would have liked to be one of those Twiggy-looking girls who could eat anything they wanted and still wear a size two. But that just wasn't the case for me.

As I have said, my general manager weighs about ninety-three pounds, and yet she often eats more than I do, and I weigh about 135 pounds. That is my normal weight, my "set-point" weight. Sometimes I may allow myself to gain or lose as much as three to five pounds, but when I do I slap myself into shape saying, "All right, get back where you belong!"

I think everybody should do that.

You should know what weight is right for you and stick to it. You may be a few pounds on either side of your ideal weight, but there should be a point that you are determined not to go past. When you get to that point, you should do something about your weight.

The goal is not just a certain weight, it's a healthy lifestyle. If you are going to stay healthy, you must set standards and limits for yourself without coming under condemnation. You have to decide that you are not going to be a slave to anything — including your body.

There Is a Limit

How shall [a person] cleanse his way? By taking heed and keeping watch [on himself] according to Your Word [conforming his life to it].

PSALM 119:9

That's what I do, and my husband does the same thing. I can guarantee you that all those who maintain their weight do that. Most of them would admit that they can't eat anything their flesh wants, anytime they want, in any amount they want. They are maintaining their weight because they are following the same principles I am sharing with you in this book. So either I am confirming that you are doing the right thing or I am showing you what you can do to get to the place you want to be — and then stay there.

I have always been a little jealous of Dave because I always felt it wasn't fair that he could eat anything he wanted to, while I always had to watch everything I ate.

One of the lessons we all have to learn is that feeling sorry for ourselves is not going to speed up our metabolism. That's too bad, but it's true. We have to quit looking at others because what works for them won't necessarily work for us. We have to set a limit on ourselves and then stick to what we know is best for us.

WISHBONE OR BACKBONE?

...God is strong, and he wants you strong.

EPHESIANS 6:10 MESSAGE

One of the managers in my ministry is married to a pretty little redhead who is real thin. I would guess that she wears about a size four. She just eats and eats and eats. She is Italian and so she eats plates of spaghetti and meatballs and pasta and all those other high-spiced dishes covered with cheese and sauce. Yet she stays the same petite size. She is also a high-energy person and is always doing something active like moving the furniture around.

Obviously, she has a high metabolism rate. I wish I did. But do you know what I have discovered? *A wishbone is not a backbone!*

YOU CAN DO IT!

...I can do everything God asks me to do with the help of Christ who gives me the strength and power.

PHILIPPIANS 4:13 TLB

No, I don't look like my ninety-three-pound general manager, and I am never going to. My metabolism is never going to be like that little redhead's. So I have got to deal with my own situation. I have got to make the most of what I have been given. I can't afford to start feeling sorry for myself or blame my problems on something that is nonexistent or unchangeable.

Some time ago I complained to my husband, "You can eat anything you want to and never gain any weight."

"Let me tell you something," he replied. "I don't eat just anything I want to. I watch what I eat all the time. I just don't say anything about it. If I start to gain a little bit of weight, I cut back on my eating until it's gone."

As you can guess, Dave is one of those silent victorious people. I am not. If I discover something that works for me, I get on my soapbox and start telling everybody in the world what they ought to do. And what I am sharing with you is the fact that something can be done about your weight problem, even if it is caused by a sluggish metabolism.

Now if you have a thyroid or other glandular problem, then get some medical help. But if you are just one of those people like me who have a slow rate of metabolism, look with me at some of the reasons for that situation and what can be done about it.

1. *Crash dieting and roller-coaster eating.*

This kind of yo-yo dieting is dangerous because it slows down the body's metabolic rate and causes it to re-accumulate fat as soon as food restraints are lifted. The more people go on yo-yo diets, the faster they regain the weight they lose each time, even if they eat less.

I never used to believe those who came to me and claimed they had been on a strict diet for weeks or months and had not lost a single pound — until I saw it happen to my daughter.

Laura came to me complaining about not being able to lose weight. I told her, "If I put you on a diet, I guarantee you will lose weight." So I designed a special diet for her and made sure she followed it to the letter. She did not lose any weight. We prayed together, and she did finally manage to lose two or three pounds, but that was all.

I knew she was not eating very much of anything, yet her weight stubbornly refused to go down. That taught me a lesson. I had always told people, "If you don't eat, you'll lose weight. If you're not losing, it's because you're eating." I learned the reason those people were not losing was that their metabolism was so far out of balance it was working to maintain their same weight — regardless of how many calories they took in.

If this is the reason for your lack of weight loss, you need to get on a regular routine of eating and follow a good exercise program. Start eating good, wholesome foods — lots of fruits, vegetables, and top-quality protein.

Properly balanced meals and sensible exercise affect the metabolism. When diet and exercise are brought into line, the metabolism begins to work better.

2. *Making excuses for overeating and eating the wrong things.*

If you really want to maintain your ideal weight and have the right size body for your frame, one of the most important things you must do is stop making excuses:

"But everybody in my family was overweight."

Yes, it is true that body size and shape do tend to follow bloodlines. In my own case, everybody in my family has a little extra in a certain spot on the body so I have to be careful to keep it exercised off all the time. My older daughter has the same problem, and so do my two sons. Our thighs are thick!

In fact, if you study families you can often see that their body sizes and shapes are about the same. But that doesn't mean they have to be excessively overweight.

"But it's just too hard!"

One time the Lord spoke to me and said, "Joyce, stop saying that everything is hard; every time you say that you make it harder."

We need to say things like, "With the help of the Holy Spirit, I can do whatever I need to do. If my metabolism doesn't work as fast as someone else's, I'll just have to watch it. I will follow the diet and exercise program the Lord has shown me to be best for me. I can do it through the power of the Holy Spirit."

Reason 6:

Spiritual Unfulfillment

Reason 6:

Spiritual Unfulfillment

*...It is written, Man shall not live and be
sustained by (on) bread alone but by
every word and expression of God.*

LUKE 4:4

═══════════════════════

I believe many people overeat simply because they
are spiritually unfulfilled. What they are experiencing is not a physical hunger, it is a spiritual hunger.

Even many Christians don't spend enough time with
God and His Word, so they feel a void which they try to
fill with food.

The next time you are roaming around the house
looking for something to eat, but you can't figure out
what you want, try prayer.

A SEARCH FOR COMFORT

And it came to pass on the fourth day, when they arose

early in the morning, that he rose up to depart: and the

damsel's father said unto his son in law, Comfort thine heart

with a morsel of bread....

JUDGES 19:5 KJV

One reason people overeat is that they are looking for comfort. They are seeking in food the love, acceptance, or fulfillment that is missing in their lives.

If a person is rooted in rejection, abuse, shame, guilt, or improper imaging from parents or other authority figures, often that individual will feel unacceptable to others and will have a poor self-image and low self-esteem.

In my own case, because of the abuse I suffered throughout my childhood, I had a very bad attitude toward others and a very poor image of myself. One way I compensated for my feelings of shame and neglect was by overeating.

Through my years of ministry I have become convinced about eighty percent of our problems today stem from the fact that for one reason or another we simply do not like ourselves.

In talking with and ministering to people I often have to tell them, "Your problem is, you do not like yourself. You have got to learn to like and accept yourself, not because of what you do or how you look, but because of who you are in Christ Jesus." (Ephesians 1:4-7.)

Please understand that losing weight has nothing to do with who you are in Christ. Overeating is a problem like any other. It is evidence of a lack of control. And when anything in our life gets out of control, it needs to be brought under the control of the Holy Spirit because it is dangerous to our health — both physical and spiritual.

SEEKING GOOD FEELINGS

O unhappy and pitiable and wretched man that I am! Who will release and deliver me from [the shackles of] this body of death?

O thank God! [He will!] through Jesus Christ (the Anointed One) our Lord!...

ROMANS 7:24,25

God has created in each of us a need to feel good about ourselves. If we are not receiving good feelings about ourselves from within, often we will look for them outside of ourselves. That's why people who have been abused, rejected, and mistreated by others, especially by those closest to them, often end up with a warped sense of self-worth that pushes them to seek approval in inappropriate ways.

It was never God's will for us to derive our sense of value and worth from outside sources such as the opinions of others. We don't need approval or affirmation from outside, we need it from within — because of who we are in Christ.

God's original plan was that man should receive his sense of value and worth from his relationship with the Father. Although that plan was disrupted by the Fall, through Christ it has been restored to us.

The problem is that too often instead of looking to God for our good feelings, we look to other sources. Some turn to alcohol to anesthetize the pain of rejection or loss or unhappiness. Others turn to drugs or even money.

The same principle applies to eating. If we do not receive the good feelings we need from within ourselves, many times we try to comfort ourselves with food. If we get upset with some problem or situation in our life, often the first thing we do is reach for something to put in our mouth. Instead, we should reach out to God for the comfort we seek.

When you are hurting inside, when you feel depressed or despondent or disturbed, don't run to the refrigerator, run to the Lord. Don't look to food to comfort you, but look to the Holy Spirit Who is the Comforter. (John 16:7).

In times like that, other people cannot provide you the comfort you need, only God can. When anything happens to bother you, if you feel tempted to turn to food for comfort, stop and pray that you will not be overcome by that temptation. If you know you have a weakness in this area, be prayerful about it. God will help you resist that temptation and overcome that weakness as you put your faith and trust in Him as your comfort and strength.

PAUL'S PROBLEM

For I do not understand my own actions [I am baffled, bewildered]. I do not practice or accomplish what I wish, but I do the very thing that I loathe [which my moral instinct condemns].

Now if I do [habitually] what is contrary to my desire, [that means that] I acknowledge and agree that the Law is good (morally excellent) and that I take sides with it.

However, it is no longer I who do the deed, but the sin [principle] which is at home in me and has possession of me.

For I know that nothing good dwells within me, that is, in my flesh. I can will what is right, but I cannot perform it. [I have the intention and urge to do what is right, but no power to carry it out.]

ROMANS 7:15-18

In this passage we see Paul was faced with the same problem that faces us today: He was unable in his flesh to overcome his basic human nature ruled by the sin principle. In verse 18 he reveals why he was not able to do the good things he wanted and willed to do but failed. It was because of a lack of power.

What Paul recognized in his own life is what we need to recognize in our life. Without the power of the Holy Ghost we are unable to resist our human nature and the pull of temptation in order to carry out the will of God for us.

JONAH'S PROBLEM

But Jonah rose up to flee to Tarshish from being in the presence of the Lord [as His prophet] and went down to Joppa and found a ship going to Tarshish [the most remote of the Phoenician trading places then known]. So he paid the appointed fare and went down into the ship to go with them to

Tarshish from being in the presence of the Lord [as His servant and minister].

JONAH 1:3

Some people may eat more than they should because they are living selfish, self-centered lives. They are trying to fulfill the call of God upon their lives through food.

When I was self-centered, I was very unhappy. And unhappy people, people who feel bad about themselves, people who are insecure and lack confidence, often eat to comfort themselves. God wants us to find our comfort in Him.

Some people may be like Jonah; they are running from God. Like Jonah, they usually end up in a terrible mess.

If you will become spiritually fulfilled, you will find that it will affect even your appetite. If you are searching to fill a void in your life through eating, shopping, television, or anything else, what you need to do is to turn to the Lord and let Him fill that void with His presence.

Reason 7:

Emotional Unfulfillment

Reason 7:

Emotional Unfulfillment

*Blessed be the God and Father of our
Lord Jesus Christ, the Father of
sympathy (pity and mercy) and the God
[Who is the Source] of every comfort
(consolation and encouragement).*

2 CORINTHIANS 1:3

---

*M*any people are overweight because they are emotionally unfulfilled. If their emotional needs are not met, they overeat to compensate.

In a marriage in which one partner is insensitive, unaffectionate, sexually unresponsive, or unfaithful, the other partner may turn to food for comfort.

Just as some married people are unable to build a healthy marital relationship, some unmarried people are unable to build a healthy social life. They may eat to try to fill that emotional void, to overcome their feelings of insecurity, their low self-esteem, their failure image.

Those who have a tremendous financial lack in their lives are never able to purchase the things that they would enjoy, so they feel deprived and eat to fill what they see as their empty lives.

EMOTIONAL NEEDS ARE REAL

Upon their return, the apostles reported to Jesus all that they had done. And He took them [along with Him] and withdrew into privacy near a town called Bethsaida.

LUKE 9:10

It is good to know that even Jesus and His disciples took time to rest and recover. I have discovered that doing things for ourselves in balance helps keep us emotionally healthy.

Every once in a while a woman may need to buy a new dress, get her nails done, and have her hair fixed. That is emotionally fulfilling to her.

Let me give you an example from my own life. When I get through ministering in a conference, I am tired. Physically, mentally, and emotionally I am drained. By the time I leave, there is nothing left in me to give to others.

I have found that when I get home I have to do something for myself; otherwise, I start feeling sorry for myself and getting angry.

For years I used to go through that process every time I left a conference. I would come away from a series of meetings where the Spirit of God had been moving in great power. Then when I got home I would act like a jerk. I began to see that the problem was that I wasn't meeting my own needs.

Sometimes we Christians like to think we don't have any needs. But God has given us the same emotions He gave everyone else.

Now after a conference I may go home and watch a classic movie on television. I may go shopping. I may call in a lady I know to give me a massage. Whatever it is, I need to do something I really enjoy.

If I don't, if I just go right back to work, sooner or later I will react emotionally. I may get mad at Dave for going golfing because he is out having fun while I am home feeling bad. If I am not careful, I will find myself roaming through the house looking for something to eat.

My problem is not my metabolism, my hormones, or anything else physical. It is purely emotional. When I behave that way, I am living an unbalanced life. I am not giving myself what I need to fill my emotional needs.

A man can have the same kind of problem. He may need to play golf, go fishing, or engage in some other activity he enjoys.

It is a known fact that a man needs to play. I know that is true because my husband will call up one of his friends and say, "Can you play today?"

Now, obviously he is taking about golf, and his friend knows that. But what he says is true nonetheless. Men need to play.

I like to play golf, but I don't need it as much as Dave does. I need to shop! It doesn't matter if I just roam around the mall and buy myself a pair of earrings, I have to meet my emotional needs.

But even then, I know that none of the things of this world — especially food — is going to permanently fill my deepest emotional needs. For that I must look not to things, but to a Person.

LOOK TO GOD, NOT FOOD

Jesus said to him, I am the Way and the Truth and the Life....

JOHN 14:6

Emotionally wounded people, those who have been abused, rejected, or abandoned by those they love, often overeat. The answer for them is the same as it is for anyone else with any other kind of emotional problem.

In 2 Corinthians 1:3 the Bible tells us that God is a Father of sympathy, pity, and mercy, the Source of every comfort, consolation, and encouragement. As His beloved children, we are to look to Him to fill our needs, not to things. If we allow Him to fill us with what we need, it will not add weight to us.

Jesus said that He is the way, the truth, and the life. That pretty much sums up the answer to every situation we may experience in this life.

For many years I was sexually abused, which left me with all kinds of problems. When we are hurt emotionally, we can run to the refrigerator, run to alcohol, run to drugs, or even run to other people, but none of that is going to permanently solve our problem. It will only dull the pain, but the wound will still be there.

Instead of running to things or to other people, we need to run to Jesus. We need to let Him love us, comfort us, console us, and encourage us. He is the God of healing and restoration.

Now I am aware that this message on twelve reasons why people overeat or become overweight may seem like a farce to you if you are suffering from long-lasting, deep-seated emotional problems. But I can honestly say that I believe with all my heart that no matter what your problem is, how long you may have suffered from it, or how deep-seated it may be, Jesus is still the answer.

Jesus is the only way to breakthrough and victory. Whatever the cause of your emotional suffering, look to Him for comfort, consolation, and encouragement.

Reason 8:

Loneliness, Loss and Boredom

Reason 8:

Loneliness, Loss and Boredom

...I came that they may have and
enjoy life, and have it in abundance
(to the full, till it overflows).

JOHN 10:10

*L*oneliness, loss, or boredom may lead to overeating. Let's look at these problems one by one so we can learn how to handle them.

DEALING WITH LONELINESS

"'...So leave the corruption and compromise; leave it for good,' says God. 'Don't link up with those who will pollute you. I want you all for myself.'"

2 CORINTHIANS 6:17 MESSAGE

It is not necessary to be alone to be lonely. If a woman is married to a man who sits and watches sports on television all the time, she may be lonely. She may end up going to the refrigerator every thirty minutes or every hour on the hour looking for something to fill the void she feels in her life.

A man may be married to a woman who spends her every free moment at the church, serving on committees and taking part in every activity. If so, he may be lonely.

Both men and women who are married to worka-
holics may be lonely.

Those who have lost a husband or a wife or those
whose children have grown and left the home may
be lonely.

If you are one of those people, don't try to fill the void
with food. Instead, you must aggressively make a new life
for yourself. That life is found only in one Source.

If you have recently accepted Jesus as your Savior
and Lord, at first you may be lonely due to your separa-
tion from wrong associations. God may be in the
process of separating you from excessive people for a
period of time to get you rooted and grounded in Him.

I went through a lot of lonely years while God was
trying to get me to realize that He was the most important thing in my life.

One time years ago I prayed, "You know, Lord, You
have just ruined me for anything else but You." What I
meant was that since coming to know the Lord intimately, nothing else in life could keep me happy or satisfied but Him.

I had become addicted to Jesus, Who is the answer
for all of life's problems.

DEALING WITH LOSS

But whatever was to my profit I now consider loss for the
sake of Christ. What is more, I consider everything a loss
compared to the surpassing greatness of knowing Christ Jesus

my Lord, for whose sake I have lost all things. I consider them rubbish, that I may gain Christ and be found in him....

PHILIPPIANS 3:7-9 NIV

Anytime we lose something of importance to us, it leaves a void in our lives that needs to be filled with something. The problem comes when we try to fill it with the wrong thing — usually food.

You may have lost a loved one, even a spouse. If so, there is a void in your life. Something that used to be there is not there anymore. In situations like that it is so very easy to turn to food for comfort.

You may have had a great job you really liked, and now for some reason you don't have it anymore. You may try to fill the void with food.

Your children may have left the home and you are suffering from the "empty-nest syndrome." If you are not careful, you may eat in an attempt to satisfy the emptiness you feel inside.

Anytime something important in our lives is taken away from us, we are going to experience a sense of loss. Sometimes we try to get back the feelings we used to enjoy through eating.

That can be dangerous.

Let me give you an example. I quit smoking more than twenty years ago. I had always been afraid to quit because I thought I would gain weight. So I used that fear as an excuse not to give up cigarettes.

When I finally stopped smoking, I did get hungry, but I was determined I was not going to try to fill that void with food. I chewed gum and drank lots of water, and after about thirty to forty days I had washed the toxins out of my body. My system began to get back into balance, and I didn't want excess food anymore.

If I had started eating as soon as I felt the first hunger pangs, I would have given up one harmful practice only to replace it with another harmful practice. I might have solved one problem, but I would have created another.

You must be very careful in this area. When God asks you to lay down one thing in your life, you must not try to compensate for the loss by filling the void with something that is going to cause you just as many problems.

You must aggressively make a new life. That new life is found only in Christ.

DEALING WITH BOREDOM

...be constantly renewed in the spirit of your mind [having a fresh mental and spiritual attitude].

EPHESIANS 4:23

Many people are bored from a lack of variety in their lives. And bored people often overeat.

This is an issue I have to deal with on a regular basis. Because I do so much of the same thing all the time, I sometimes have to fight boredom.

When I go to speak at a conference, for example, it is a new and exciting thing to those who attend. For them, it is a welcome break from their ordinary routine. But for me, it is the same thing I have been doing all year long. I may have held fifteen such conferences that same month.

Because of that situation I have to stick really close to God and allow Him to keep the sense of excitement in my life that would not be there naturally.

We who are in the ministry have made a commitment to lay down our lives to serve others, and we are glad to do so. But the truth is, we are as human as anyone else. We get just as tired, just as worn down, just as bored as those to whom we minister.

Sometimes we deal so much in the spiritual realm that when we do have time to do something in the natural realm, we don't know what to do with ourselves.

For Christians it is often hard to find good, wholesome entertainment. There are not many movies we can go see, not many parties we can attend, not many plays or other shows we can enjoy. I once had to get up and leave an opera because of the vulgar language being used on stage.

That kind of thing really aggravates me. It seems that Satan is out to ruin everything in this world that God's people really enjoy so they will become bored and not know what to do with themselves except eat.

I really believe that is why so many of us Christians are overweight. We simply can't find anything clean and wholesome to do, so we turn to food, figuring it is not a sin. It may not be a sin, but it certainly can be a trap of the enemy to destroy us and our witness for the Lord.

BOREDOM EQUALS THE BULGE!

And the Lord God planted a garden toward the east, in Eden [delight]; and there He put the man whom He had formed (framed, constituted).

And out of the ground the Lord God made to grow every tree that is pleasant to the sight or to be desired — good (suitable, pleasant) for food....

GENESIS 2:8,9

When God created the earth, He made all kinds of wonderful things for the delight of man and gave them to him to enjoy freely. So besides liberty, the Holy Spirit also likes variety. If we follow Him instead of some prescribed, regimented program, we will not end up bored.

In one of my notes on this subject of blindly following self-imposed dietary rules and regulations I wrote, *"Boredom equals the bulge."*

Often we become bored with following the same program, eating the same foods at the same time, so we end up dissatisfied — or perhaps just unsatisfied. We think we want more food, when what we are really craving is a wider variety of food.

The same principle applies to prayer and every other aspect of our lives. We must learn to keep ourselves from coming under law because it does not lead to the freedom the Holy Spirit wants us to have and enjoy as the children of God.

Beware of boredom. Learn to conquer it by keeping variety in your life, including a variety of foods, and by relying on the power and presence of the Lord.

Reason 9:

Preoccupation With Food

Reason 9:

Preoccupation With Food

*...Take no thought for your life,
what ye shall eat....*

MATTHEW 6:25 KJV

*A*nother reason for overeating is thinking about food all the time. Keeping the mind on food stirs up the appetite.

This is another area in which I have to be careful. I am not sure why it is such an issue with me, but I think it is because I spent so many years on diets in my younger days.

My husband does not think about food until he gets hungry. But if I am not careful, I will be thinking about my next meal before I have finished the one I am eating at the time. Sometimes while I am eating one meal, I will actually be planning the next.

I am sure that I am not alone in that respect.

Part of the reason we tend to think about eating all the time is that in our society we are bombarded with images of food. Everywhere we look today we see television commercials, billboard advertisements, magazine layouts filled with pictures of enticing things to eat and drink. If we go to the movie, we can smell the popcorn before we even get through the front door.

In today's world, it takes a very determined person to avoid giving in to the temptation to eat and become overweight.

THINKING AND OVEREATING

Therefore let anyone who thinks he stands [who feels sure that he has a steadfast mind and is standing firm], take heed lest he fall [into sin].

1 CORINTHIANS 10:12

Thinking has a lot to do with eating. If we think about food all the time, we are as controlled by it as we would be if we ate it constantly.

One time the Lord gave me a statement which I think summarizes this whole point: *"Lust is birthed in undisciplined thinking."*

Take adultery, for example. Do two people just fall into an adulterous relationship without any thought on their part? No, adulterous affairs don't happen that way. There is usually a lot of wrong thinking that goes on before the wrong action.

The same is true in eating. One of the things you and I must do is ask God to help us discipline our mind so it is not on food all the time.

If you know you have a tendency to use food for comfort, and you have an argument with your spouse and start thinking about food as a release for your pent-up tension, you need to do something before it gets out of control. Instead of sitting and thinking about eating, go out and do something active. Mow the yard or weed the flower bed, play a game of tennis or golf, or just take a walk around the block a couple of times — anything to get your mind off food. Because if you sit and brood, sooner or later you will likely end up eating to comfort your unsettled emotions.

Another example of undisciplined thinking involves television viewing. We all know we can be sitting and watching TV with no thought of eating at all. Suddenly on the screen will flash an image of some tempting food, and the next minute we are thinking what a great idea it would be to go to the kitchen and fix ourselves something tasty to eat. That's when we have to exercise right thinking and will power. The best way to resist that kind of temptation is by getting our thoughts on something else.

Appetite, like many other desires, is normal. The problem comes when we allow it to get out of control. And that usually happens as a result of wrong thinking. As we are told by the apostle Paul, we need to pay attention to our thinking and take heed lest we fall into temptation and sin.

Our problem is often basically just a lack of mental discipline, which can only come through total commitment to the Word and will of God in reliance on His indwelling Holy Spirit.

Reason 10:

Impulse Eating

Reason 10:
Impulse Eating

...The eye is not satisfied with seeing....
ECCLESIASTES 1:8

*M*any people overeat simply because the food is there in front of their eyes, and they can't seem to resist it. They think they have to taste everything they see.

My son once told me that one of the hardest things he ever had to do was to learn not to snatch up something to eat when he came into my house.

If he came in and saw a plate of cookies or an open bag of potato chips on the kitchen counter, he would almost unconsciously reach out and grab a few and stick them in his mouth, just because they were there for the taking.

Be very careful about impulse eating. Don't just grab something up and stuff it into your mouth. If you get in the habit of eating without even realizing what you are doing, you may end up finding yourself overweight and not know why.

ORDINARY IMPULSES OF THE FLESH

However, brethren, I could not talk to you as to spiritual [men], but as to nonspiritual [men of the flesh, in whom the carnal nature predominates], as to mere infants [in the new life] in Christ [unable to talk yet!]

I fed you with milk, not solid food, for you were not yet strong enough [to be ready for it]; but even yet you are not strong enough [to be ready for it],

For you are still [unspiritual, having the nature] of the flesh *[under the control of ordinary impulses]*....

1 CORINTHIANS 3:1-3

As Christians we ought to be mature enough by now to be able to distinguish between the leading of the Holy Spirit within us and the ridiculous demands made on us by our carnal flesh — what the Bible refers to as "ordinary impulses of the flesh." Impulses obeyed over and over become compulsion.

Imagine you are in the mall shopping and you spot a red sale tag on an article you would love to have. Suddenly you get an impulse to buy it though you know it is not what you went there to buy at all. You struggle within because your emotions are telling you that you just have to have it, it's on sale, and you will never have such an opportunity again.

It is amazing how much pain you can avoid in situations like that by just taking a little time to back away and think before acting.

That is an example of what the Bible is talking about when it warns against coming under the control of ordinary impulses. That is a temptation we must all learn to resist for our own good — so we can have what we *really* want most.

SELECTIVE EATING

So then, whether you eat or drink, or whatever you may do, do all for the honor and glory of God.

1 CORINTHIANS 10:31

Many times our problem is simply eating what is before us or easy rather than selective eating.

In my ministry I travel a great deal by air. It is so easy for people on airplanes to eat whatever is put in front of them, and many people do. Even if we aren't hungry, we can gobble down snacks like peanuts or cheese-flavored chips as though we are starving, simply because we are served them. Many of those snacks have no real food value and are sometimes laden with calories, fat, cholesterol, and sodium, yet it is easy to eat them without thinking simply because they are set before us.

One time the Lord spoke to one of our staff members and told her, "You eat anything that anybody sticks under your nose without even stopping to think whether you want it or not."

This happened right after this young woman had been to her sister's house one night and had eaten a piece of cake she really didn't want just because it was set in front of her by her brother-in-law.

After it was gone, she asked herself, "Why did I eat that piece of cake?" The Lord spoke to her and said,

"Because you are passive about your eating. You should be selective."

What God spoke to her, He is speaking to you and me today. He is telling us we need to give more thought to what is set before us or what we pick up and stick in our mouth simply because it is available to us.

We must take charge of our body. We must be careful to keep it in proper working condition, because it is the vehicle we use to carry out the work God has given us to accomplish on this earth.

Ask the Lord to help you keep your impulses under control of your better judgment so you can eat selectively.

Reason 11:

Passive Eating

Reason 11:

Passive Eating

*The slothful man does not catch his game
or roast it once he kills it....*

PROVERBS 12:27

Many people are overweight simply because of the time and effort it takes to be fit and trim.

It requires effort to carefully shop for the right kinds of foods and then properly prepare them. For some people, especially those with growing children and busy schedules, following a balanced eating program may require fixing different meals for the rest of family and for themselves. That takes effort. It also takes effort to exercise regularly and get the right amounts of rest and recreation.

There are other people who are just plain lazy and won't put out the effort to do these things! They will simply follow the course of least resistance, many times because of repeated failure in trying different diets, and go on complaining and making excuses about their weight. They don't realize, or have given up hope, there is a way to control it.

THE REAL REASONS FOR BEING OVERWEIGHT

For you, brethren, were [indeed] called to freedom; only
[do not let your] freedom be an incentive to your flesh and an
opportunity or excuse [for selfishness]....

GALATIANS 5:13

We have seen that we must be on our guard against
using our spiritual freedom as an incentive to satisfy our
fleshly desires. We have also seen that we must be on
our guard against making excuses for not taking control
over our eating and weight, such as, "My metabolism
works slower than other people's."

We have seen that although it is true that each of us
has a different rate of metabolism, individual rates can
be brought into balance and made to function at the
optimum rate by proper eating and exercise.

Now let's consider some of the other excuses we
often make for our eating and weight problems.

1. *"My Clothes Are Shrinking!"*

The last time I gained weight, I first tried to blame
the problem on my clothes rather than on my size.
When I would put on a dress or skirt that had become
too tight, I would complain to my husband, "What is
the lady who does the laundry doing to my clothes? Is
she throwing them in the dryer and shrinking them?"

If I put on a piece of clothing that had been sent to
the cleaners, I would gripe to Dave, "What are those

people at the cleaners doing to my clothes? They're shrinking them!"

Later I got on the scales and saw I had gained about seven pounds. Suddenly it hit me. The problem was not that my clothes were getting smaller, it was that I was getting bigger!

2. *"Everything I Eat Goes to Fat!"*

Another popular excuse we make is: "I hardly eat anything, and yet I still gain weight. Everything I eat goes to fat!"

The truth is that we usually eat more than we think we do. I learned that lesson years ago when the Lord put me on a ten-day partial fast.

One of the things God revealed to me through that fast was how much food I really was eating each day — especially by "forking," which can be very deceptive.

Until I went on that partial fast and had to pay strict attention to everything that went into my mouth, I had not realized how often I was snatching bits and pieces of food from sources other than the table.

For example, when I would go to the refrigerator to get a piece of cheese for my children, I would usually break it in half and give one part to them and eat the other part myself. I never counted those kinds of "sneak snacks" in my eating. If I did that eight or ten times a week, you can see how much cheese I was eating without counting it as part of my diet.

I would also take things from the plates of my husband and children or eat directly out of pie or cake pans without considering the number of calories I was consuming. Since I did not call that eating, I was not taking it into account when I figured up my total calorie intake for the week.

What I discovered was that when I said I hardly ate anything at all, I was deceiving myself. I was eating much more than I realized. I also had to face the fact that everything I ate did not go to fat, it just went into my body which took it and stored the excess as fat! As my daughter said recently, "Mom, we have to face it. Everything we put in our mouths counts!"

3.   *"I Can't Help It!"*

Often we say things like, "I can't help it, my nerves make me eat." Of course, we know that is not so. We eat because we choose to eat, not because our nerves dictate to us.

Or we may say, "I can't help it, I have low blood sugar and have to eat every two hours." That may be so, but if we would eat the right foods every two hours, it would keep our blood sugar level in balance without making us gain weight.

Or we may say, "I can't help it, I just gain weight easily." Again, that may be true. But that is why we need to eat the right foods in the right amount — so we won't gain weight so easily.

Finally, we may try to lay the blame on something else in our life, like tobacco: "I can't help it, I quit smoking, and it made me eat." Circle that word "it." As long as we blame something or someone other than ourselves for our eating, we are going to go on being overweight and having troubles with our health.

The truth many of us ought to realize is: "I am overweight because I take in more calories than my body burns up. I eat the wrong things in the wrong amount. I have been on the feast and famine cycle so long my body's metabolism is mixed up so that it cannot operate correctly. I have to go through a period of treating my body right so that it will begin to function properly for me again."

Once people realize the "obvious" reasons they thought they were overweight are not the true reasons, they have hope that they really can lose weight. The truth helps to give them new determination once they realize they really can be free.

With the help of the Lord you can bring your eating and weight under control. You will feel much better physically — and much better about yourself.

Reason 12:

Lack of Self-Denial

Reason 12:

Lack of Self-Denial

*And Jesus called [to Him] the throng
with His disciples and said to them,
If anyone intends to come after Me,
let him deny himself....*

MARK 8:34

Finally, many people overeat because they are not willing to deny themselves.

Some time ago our son Danny lost sixty-five pounds. We did not even know he was trying to lose weight. He has been big all his life. He is six feet five inches tall and wears a size fourteen shoe, so he is just a naturally large young man.

But although he had been chunky all his life, his father and I started noticing that he was losing weight so we asked him about it. He admitted that he had been on a diet. He just kept on losing and losing until he had lost the full amount he wanted to take off.

Curious about how he managed to stay on his diet so well, I asked him, "Dan, don't you ever get hungry?"

"Yeah, sure I do," he answered.

"What do you do about it?" I asked.

"Nothing," he replied. "It passes."

Someone else who needed to lose weight overheard him say that and told me later, "What Danny said helped me more than anything I have heard in a long time. I realized that just because people are thin doesn't mean they never get hungry. It just means they have learned to say no to themselves and are willing to feel uncomfortable sometimes."

Although Danny lost sixty-five pounds, it was not always easy. There were times when he had to deny himself, times when he had to be willing to be uncomfortable for a while.

REASONS VERSUS EXCUSES

I turned about [penitent] and my heart was set to know and to search out and to seek [true] wisdom and the reason of things....

ECCLESIASTES 7:25

Reasons are totally different from excuses. A reason is what has caused us to be the way we are; an excuse is what keeps us that way.

Some of us are overweight because we were abused in our childhood, and we compensated by overeating.

Some of us are overweight because we grew up in poverty and never had enough to eat, so now that we have plenty we overindulge.

Some of us are overweight because we were not popular or well liked or because we felt inferior or unloved, so we eat for the comfort that food provides.

All of these reasons for overeating or being overweight are valid, but if we are not careful they can become excuses for staying the way we are.

THE TRUTH SETS YOU FREE

And you will know the Truth, and the Truth will set you free.

JOHN 8:32

As we saw before, Jesus has promised us if we really want to know the truth, we will know it, and it will set us free. We need to spend time with God, asking Him to reveal to us the reason we overeat, not so we can excuse our behavior but so we can be set free from whatever it is that is causing it.

However, for some people reasons do become excuses. Let me give you an example from my own life.

REASON IS NO EXCUSE

Come now, and let us reason together, says the Lord. Though your sins are like scarlet, they shall be as white as snow; though they are red like crimson, they shall be like wool.

If you are willing and obedient, you shall eat the good of the land.

ISAIAH 1:18,19

Because I was abused, mistreated, and controlled throughout my childhood, I grew up with a very bad attitude and outlook. I felt sorry for myself, got depressed on a regular basis, and was extremely judgmental and temperamental. If things didn't go just as I wanted them to, I would throw a fit. I blamed everything that went wrong on my upbringing, claiming, "I am the way I am because of the way I was treated."

Before I could get the victory over my situation, one of the things the Lord had to get across to me loud and clear was this truth: "Yes, that is the reason you are the way you are, but it is no excuse to stay that way!"

That truth eventually set me free.

THE CHOICE IS YOURS!

I call heaven and earth to witness this day...that I have set before you life and death, the blessings and the curses; therefore choose life, that you and your descendants may live.

DEUTERONOMY 30:19

One time a young lady who works in our ministry said to me, "God told me it's not my fault that I am the way I am."

My answer was, "That may be true. It may not be your fault that you are the way you are, but it is your fault if you stay that way."

I did not mean for that statement to sound harsh. I just believed it was necessary for me to say it in order to help her avoid the deception of using her reason for being the way she was as an excuse for staying that way.

I know how the flesh is. All of us look for something to latch onto in an attempt to avoid our responsibility for change. While God may assure us that the way we are is not our fault, He will never allow us to shift our responsibility for changing.

In my case, the Lord said to me, "Joyce, I am not saying you don't have a reason to feel sorry for yourself. Anybody who was treated as you were has every *reason* to feel bad. But you have no *right* to do so, because I am willing to set you free. **You can be pitiful or you can be powerful.** The choice is up to you."

WHICH WILL IT BE?

But the word is very near you, in your mouth and in your mind and in your heart, so that you can do it.

See, I have set before you this day life and good, and death and evil.

[If you obey the commandments of the Lord your God which] I command you today...then you shall live and multiply, and the Lord your God will bless you....

DEUTERONOMY 30:14-16

In this part of this book we have examined some of the reasons for the eating disorders that plague so many of us. Hopefully, by doing so we have gained some understanding of the truth so we can be set free.

After you have read this section, get in agreement with yourself that no matter how many reasons God shows you for the way you are, you are going to rejoice in that truth, but you are not going to allow those reasons to become excuses for staying as you are.

Reasons are what got us into bondage. Excuses are what keep us in bondage. Truth is what sets us free — if we face it, accept it, and then act on it. We will never make any progress in overcoming our eating and weight problems until we take personal responsibility for them.

If you have seen yourself in this section, ask the Lord to reveal to you what you are to do about your situation. Then be responsible enough to do what He reveals to you with faith that doing the Word of Truth will indeed set you free.

If you are willing to deny yourself, even when it means being uncomfortable, if you have the willpower to eat the right things and the determination to follow a sensible exercise program, you are on your way to solving your eating and weight problems.

Conclusion:

God's Plan for Eating

Conclusion:

God's Plan for Eating

*For I know the thoughts and plans
that I have for you, says the Lord,
thoughts and plans for welfare and
peace and not for evil, to give you
hope in your final outcome.*

JEREMIAH 29:11

*M*ost diets fail because they are built on the starvation principle. They deny the body the nourishment it needs to maintain health and vitality. Whenever the body is deprived of its basic requirements, sooner or later it begins to rebel and demand what it needs to perform properly. The result is often the feast and famine cycle — which is why any weight lost is quickly regained.

That is not God's plan.

DO IT GOD'S WAY!

Teach me Your way, O Lord, and lead me in a plain and even path....

PSALM 27:11

God has a plan for everything in life, and that plan works whether the person who follows it is saved or unsaved. For example, the principle of sowing and reaping, ...*For whatever a man sows, that and that only is what he will reap* (Galatians 6:7), works for the unbeliever as well as for the believer.

The same is true for eating. If we really want to maintain proper weight and reap the benefits of good health that go with it, we must eat according to God's plan. There is no other permanent solution, there are only temporary "fixes" that often end in misery and frustration.

I know of many people who spend large amounts of time and money following various fad diets in a desperate attempt to lose excess weight. Although they may lose for a while, invariably they gain back what they have lost — and often even more.

It is a vicious cycle.

I know of one lady who went on a liquid diet and over a period of time lost sixty or seventy pounds. Some time later I ran into her out shopping, and she had gained back every bit of the weight she had lost.

Why did that happen? It happened because in all her dieting she had not really learned good eating habits. She was not nourishing her body properly. By denying her body what it needed for health and energy, she was literally starving it. As soon as she quit starving and started back eating, she gained back everything she had lost. As so often happens, soon she was right back out of control in her eating.

That is the usual dieting cycle: starvation to lack of control. That is not only frustrating, it is also dangerous. It is not God's way.

LISTEN BEFORE EATING

And your ears will hear a word behind you, saying, This is the way; walk in it, when you turn to the right hand and when you turn to the left.

ISAIAH 30:21

Whether we eat the wrong things or overeat because we are out of control, or because we have some kind of emotional fear of going hungry, or because of some other psychological or spiritual problem, the underlying reason is still the same. We have been programmed wrong when it comes to eating. We need to be reprogrammed according to God's plan and will for us.

The way we reprogram ourselves in this area is by spending time with God before each meal and listening to Him before we start eating. By that I don't mean we have to go off somewhere and get down on our knees and pray before we put anything in our mouth. But we do need to be mindful of the Holy Spirit within us and learn to communicate with Him about what and how much we are to eat.

DEALING WITH TEMPTATION

And lead us not into temptation, but deliver us from evil....

MATTHEW 6:13 KJV

In own modern food-conscious society, there is no way to avoid food or the temptation that often comes with it. Jesus has told us that in this world temptation must come. (John 16:33.) That's why He also told us to pray that we enter not into temptation. (Luke 22:40,46.) He knew that although our spirit may be willing to resist the temptation of wrong eating, our flesh is weak in this area. (Matthew 26:41.)

If you are tired of being in bondage, resist the temptation to following the rules and regulations of diets and the desires of the flesh, which are often to eat what you don't even want! Learn to depend upon the power of the Holy Spirit within you to help you resist the ordinary impulses of your carnal nature so that you can choose what your body really wants and needs.

God wants to set us free from our self-imposed bondage, but He has to wait until we reach the point of truly listening to Him. Now that I have been set free, I am able to help many others who are going through the same things I endured for so long.

The lesson we all need to learn is that depriving ourselves is not the answer. It only leads to temptation — and all the misery that goes with it.

You Shall be Satisfied with Good Things

The meek shall eat and be satisfied: they shall praise the Lord that seek him: your heart shall live for ever.

PSALM 22:26 KJV

The truth of the matter is, we are going to end up eating one way or another. If we do it properly, we won't feel deprived, our body will burn off what we eat at a normal rate of speed, and eventually our weight will come down to the level that is right for us.

If you are overweight and you begin to eat what God created, keeping in touch with your body which is under the control of His Holy Spirit and not your carnal nature, you will discover you can eat anything you *really* want and still stay thin. And you won't go around feeling hungry or deprived or sorry for yourself. When I get hungry, if I just go and stick something in my mouth, it can often be the wrong thing — something that does not satisfy me for long. Then I end up eating something else. But if I take a minute to ponder about what I really want, then go eat it, I stay satisfied. When I am really hungry, my flesh may want a big greasy hamburger with all the trimmings. But a minute of proper thought often lets me know I would really rather have a turkey sandwich on whole wheat bread with lettuce, tomato, red onion, fat-free mayonnaise and mustard.

Most of the time you will find if you take normal portions of good nutritious food, you will be satisfied. You won't feel hungry or uncomfortable, because you will be eating the right things in the right amount.

If you make right choices, you will be happier and healthier. You won't feel miserable because you have deprived yourself then gone on a binge. You will have learned to control your weight because you can control your "ordinary impulses." You will have learned to eat and stay thin, and because of that freedom, you are ready to open yourself to God to receive all the good He is ready to give you!

Victory and Freedom
for You!

Victory and Freedom
for You!

*I*n closing I would like to say that I sincerely believe you can do this — you can experience victory to be free from spending your life in a constant struggle with food. If you have had long-standing problems in this area, I want you to know I have compassion for you. I believe you can apply the simple, practical principles in this book and reach the weight that is right for you. I have set myself in agreement in prayer with others that those who read this book will break through into victory in this area of bondage, through the truth the Holy Spirit reveals to them and through His power.

I encourage you not to choose a goal weight that is below what your body structure will handle well. Some people want to look like someone else whose size they admire, but the fact is we are not meant to be someone else. God will help us be all He has intended us to be — at the right weight for our size and frame.

You may have tried all kinds of diets and programs in the past, and bought this book hoping you had found a new "diet" that might work for you. I believe you have! You have found God's diet: good, sensible, healthy, Spirit-led eating mixed with a proper amount of exercise. I am sure the diet industry takes in millions, if not billions, of dollars each year. It is interesting to see that God has included in His Book (the Bible) all the instruction we need to weigh what He wants us to weigh — the right weight for us.

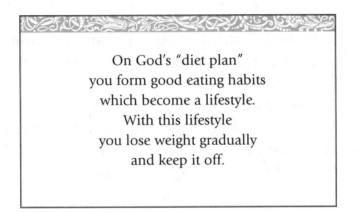

On God's "diet plan"
you form good eating habits
which become a lifestyle.
With this lifestyle
you lose weight gradually
and keep it off.

We frequently look for answers everywhere else before we discover that God had our answer all the time. There are some programs available today that teach people these same principles except in a little different way. If being part of a group helps you, and you really feel it is what God wants for you, go for it! The main point I had on my heart to make when writing this book was to teach people they can be *free* in this area — eternal dieting is bondage, and God sent Jesus to set us free! Remember that God originally told Adam and Eve they could *freely* eat. I don't think His original plan has changed. He wants each of us to be free to enjoy the good things He has provided for us, but He does not want us to be controlled by them.

I have already prayed that each person who reads this book will be affected by it in a very positive way. I have prayed for you, that through God's power, these principles will work for you, that you will experience the joy of freedom in this area.

Let's join our prayers in agreement that the many people who so need to be free from the bondage of struggling with food will finally be set free to reach and maintain the weight God desires for them. They will be free to go on to reach the heights God has planned for them — to become all God intends for them to be!

*Prayer for
a Personal Relationship
With the Lord*

Prayer for a Personal Relationship With the Lord

*G*od wants you to receive His free gift of salvation. Jesus wants to save you and fill you with the Holy Spirit more than anything. If you have never invited Jesus, the Prince of Peace, to be your Lord and Savior, I invite you to do so now. Pray the following prayer, and if you are really sincere about it, you will experience a new life in Christ.

Father,

You loved the world so much, You gave Your only begotten Son to die for our sins so that whoever believes in Him will not perish, but have eternal life.

Your Word says we are saved by grace through faith as a gift from You. There is nothing we can do to earn salvation.

I believe and confess with my mouth that Jesus Christ is Your Son, the Savior of the world. I believe He died on the cross for me and bore all of my sins, paying the price for them. I believe in my heart that You raised Jesus from the dead.

I ask You to forgive my sins. I confess Jesus as my Lord. According to Your Word, I am saved and will spend eternity

*with You! Thank You, Father. I am so grateful! In Jesus'
name, amen.*

See John 3:16; Ephesians 2:8,9; Romans 10:9,10; 1 Corinthians
15:3,4; 1 John 1:9; 4:14-16; 5:1,12,13.

Prayer for
Freedom From Bondage to Food

*F*ather, I come to You in the mighty name of Jesus Christ. I know that Jesus paid the sacrifice that we might be free, and I know that You want every one of us to be free to eat and stay thin. You want us to be able to sit down to a meal and eat without fear of becoming fat from what we eat.

I am free by the power of Your Word. I believe You will give me the strength to do what I now know to do in order to break free from the bondages that have been holding me back from all the beautiful things You have planned for me. I thank You that I am free by the blood of Jesus and the sacrifice that He made on the cross of Calvary. Thank You for making me free through the truth of Your Word and for empowering me with Your power, strength and wisdom to eat and stay thin! Help me weigh what You want me to weigh and be all You want me to be. In Jesus' name, amen.

References

Allison, Kathleen Cahill. *American Medical Association Complete Guide to Women's Health*. New York: Random House, 1996.

Edlin, Gordon, Golanty, Gordon. *Health and Wellness*. Boston: Jones and Bartlett, 1992.

Epps, Roselyn P., Stewart, Susan C. medical eds. *The Women's Complete Healthbook/The American Women's Association*. New York: Delacorte Press; Bantam Doubleday Dell Publishing Group, Inc., 1995.

The Good Health Fact Book. Pleasantville, New York: The Reader's Digest Association, 1992.

Goor, Ron, Goor, Nancy, Boyd, Katherine, *The Choose To Lose Diet*. Boston: Houghton Mifflin Company, 1990.

Larson, David E. ed. *Mayo Clinic Family Health Book*. William Morrow and Company, Inc., 1996.

Sharkey, Brian J. *Physiology of Fitness*. Champaign: Human Kinetics Books, 1990.

Endnotes

CHAPTER 1
[1] Matthew 26:41

PART 2
REASON 1
[1] Based on *The Women's Complete Healthbook*, p. 49.
[2] *Mayo Clinic Family Health Book*, p. 278.

REASON 3
[1] *Mayo Clinic Family Health Book*, p. 278.
[2] Based on information in *The Women's Complete Healthbook*, p. 39; *Mayo Clinic Family Health Book*, p. 290; *Physiology of Fitness*, p. 9.

REASON 5
[1] *Mayo Clinic Family Health* Book, p. 258.
[2] Based on *The Women's Complete Healthbook*, p. 49.
[3] *Microsoft Bookself '95, Encyclopedia*, s.v. "hypothalamus."
[4] Information in the preceding three paragraphs is based on *Health and Wellness*, p. 134.

About the Author

*J*oyce **Meyer** has been teaching the Word of God since 1976 and in full-time ministry since 1980. As an associate pastor at Life Christian Center in St. Louis, Missouri, she developed, coordinated and taught a weekly meeting known as "Life In The Word." After more than five years, the Lord brought it to a conclusion, directing her to establish her own ministry and call it "Life In The Word, Inc."

Joyce's "Life In The Word" radio broadcast is heard on more than 216 stations nationwide. Joyce's 30-minute "Life In The Word With Joyce Meyer" television program was released in 1993 and is broadcast throughout the United States and several foreign countries. Her teaching tapes are enjoyed internationally. She travels extensively conducting Life In The Word conferences, as well as speaking in local churches.

Joyce and her husband, Dave, business administrator at Life In The Word, have been married over 31 years and are the parents of four children. Three are married, and their youngest son resides with them in Fenton, Missouri, a St. Louis suburb.

Joyce believes the call on her life is to establish believers in God's Word. She says, "Jesus died to set the captives free, and far too many Christians have little or no victory in their daily lives." Finding herself in the same situation many years ago, and having found freedom to live in victory through applying God's Word,

Joyce goes equipped to set captives free and to exchange *ashes for beauty.*

Joyce has taught on emotional healing and related subjects in meetings all over the country, helping hundreds of thousands. She has recorded more than 175 different audiocassette albums and is the author of 31 books to help the Body of Christ on various topics.

Her "Emotional Healing Package" contains over 23 hours of teaching on the subject. Albums included in this package are: "Confidence"; "Beauty for Ashes" (includes a syllabus); "Managing Your Emotions"; "Bitterness, Resentment, and Unforgiveness"; "Root of Rejection"; and a 90-minute Scripture/music tape entitled, "Healing the Brokenhearted."

Joyce's "Mind Package" features five different audio tape series on the subject of the mind. They include: "Mental Strongholds and Mindsets"; "Wilderness Mentality"; "The Mind of the Flesh"; "The Wandering, Wondering Mind"; and "Mind, Mouth, Moods & Attitudes." The package also contains Joyce's powerful 260-page book, *Battlefield of the Mind.* On the subject of love she has two tape series entitled, "Love Is..." and "Love: The Ultimate Power."

Write to Joyce Meyer's office for a resource catalog and further information on how to obtain the tapes you need to bring total healing to your life.

To contact the author write:

Joyce Meyer
Life In The Word, Inc.
P. O. Box 655
Fenton, Missouri 63026
or call:
(314) 349-0303

*Please include your testimony
or help received from this
book when you write.
Your prayer requests are welcome.*

To contact the author in Canada,
please write:
Joyce Meyer Ministries Canada, Inc.
P. O. Box 2995
London, ON N6A 4H9

In Australia, please write:
Joyce Meyer Ministries-Australia
Locked Bag 77
Mansfield Delivery Centre
Queensland 4122
or call:
(07) 3349 1200

Books By Joyce Meyer

Eat and Stay Thin

Weary Warriors, Fainting Saints

Life in the Word Devotional

*Be Anxious for Nothing — The Art of Casting Your Cares
and Resting in God*

The Help Me! Series:
I'm Alone!
I'm Stressed! • I'm Insecure! • I'm Discouraged!
I'm Depressed! • I'm Worried! • I'm Afraid!

*Don't Dread — Overcoming the Spirit of Dread
With the Supernatural Power of God*

*Managing Your Emotions
Instead of Your Emotions Managing You*

Life in the Word (Quotes)

Healing the Brokenhearted

"Me and My Big Mouth!"

Prepare To Prosper

Do It! Afraid

Expect a Move of God in Your Life...Suddenly

*Enjoying Where You Are On the Way
to Where You Are Going*

*The Most Important Decision
You'll Ever Make*

When, God, When?

Why, God, Why?

The Word, The Name, The Blood

Battlefield of the Mind

Tell Them I Love Them

Peace

The Root of Rejection

Beauty for Ashes

If Not for the Grace of God

By Dave Meyer

Nuggets of Life

Available from your local bookstore.

Harrison House
Tulsa, Oklahoma 74153

The Harrison House Vision

Proclaiming the truth and the power
Of the Gospel of Jesus Christ
With excellence;

Challenging Christians to
Live victoriously,
Grow spiritually,
Know God intimately.